Should I Stay or Should I go?

From Relationship Clash to CLARITY in 5 simple steps.

By Matt Albiges.

First Edition
ISBN: 978-1-7385526-0-3

Any references to historical events, real people or real places are used fictitiously, and all names are the product of the author's imagination. Information and resources are based on the author's personal experience. The author assumes no responsibility or liability whatsoever for action taken as a consequence of reading this book.

Book cover design by: IdeAde

First printed edition 2024.

Published by Aligned Resources Ltd, Cardiff UK.
www.alignedwithlove.net

Acknowledgements

I would like to start by sharing my gratitude to the many people who have made this book a reality.

To our incredible team at Aligned Resources, for your passionate support to Rebeca and myself as we've shared our work and brought this book to life.

To the clients that we've worked with I salute your sincerity in reaching out for support and believing that a better relationship is possible, and thank you for putting your faith in us to guide you to that place.

We've been supported by our families and friends – many of whom have provided comments and feedback in the creation of this book.

To our own mentors and teachers that have believed in us and supported us - we could not have done this without you!

Contents

Introduction

Dedication

This book is dedicated to everyone who has ever woken up - in a cold sweat in the middle of the night - to realise that whatever the costs may have been of their relationship up until that point, that something must change and that better is possible.

Remember that whatever you decide to do to resolve your relationship challenges, you are only ever one decision away from a completely different life.

Reaching for another level

We may not yet have met, though I believe that you have picked up this book for a reason. That reason is somehow linked to the motivation that made me set off on this journey of understanding and wanting to finally resolve my own struggling long-term relationship. I knew that there was more, and I was committed to doing whatever it took to find that next level.

The fact that you are reading this book shows that we are on some level united in that journey of change, even if for now we may be in different stages of our journeys. My purpose in authoring this book is to support people who want to consider taking a step forward of their journey to a different and better tomorrow. While it's focussed on solving our relationship challenge, many clients report improvements in other areas of their lives through undertaking this journey such as at work or in parenting.

Let me start by honouring that drive and belief that while we may not yet have the answer, that an answer is there for discovering. Also, in committing that as we go on this journey together that your understanding of your relationship will be vastly different by the end of it. Whatever you consider to be your goal, I invite you to think big. While small incremental change could be an important stepping stone, we have the opportunity of accessing something fundamental where we could look back one day at the journey we've been on with wonder and awe. What a different life we've created, we may reflect, and all because we started with a dream of what could be possible, and that we took the first step in picking up this book.

Preface - a wake-up call

It's early evening and I'm already in bed. Working away from home in a new job, I feel that I need to show up in the office even though with the virus that I'm struggling with I would have probably been better advised to rest in bed. I am recovering from the exertion of pushing through the exhaustion barrier to show up as best I could with my new colleagues. Now safely back at home, pulling the cover over my head, and with a hot water bottle tucked under my arm I'm feeling better just allowing my body to be, as it fights off whatever infection I've picked up.

My phone rings and I check and it's my partner calling.

I guess she's worried about me, I think. She knows that I'm unwell. A short conversation might make me feel a bit better anyway - and perhaps there's a domestic issue or household problem that I need to know about.

She gets straight to the point.

"Right, I'm sorry about that - yeah, that must have been quite inconvenient for you!" It turns out that she needed some detail from a correspondence that I'd passed on which was incomplete.

"Yes, I can check on that later, but I'll need to get my laptop which is downstairs, and I'm feeling really rough in bed... would it be ok if I look that up for you in the morning?"

"No ok, but I didn't do it on purpose..."

"Ok but that doesn't make me a bad person, does it...?"

The line goes dead.

As I put my phone down and collapse back into my bed holding my hot water bottle, I allow the feelings from this conversation to sit with me for a moment.

From the start of the conversation to the end, my partner didn't at any point ask how I was feeling, to ask how she could support or make any allowance or consideration for my illness. Her only interest was to make a point out of my lack of attention, and to highlight my lack thereof.

Is this really what my relationship has come to? Is there ANY love in this relationship at all, I wonder.

While this wasn't the first time we'd had a challenging interaction - in fact, things had been difficult for years - there was something about my weakened state, letting go and recognising my powerlessness at that moment that made it land in on a deeper level.

"Is this going to be the "loving relationship" that I am going to experience for the rest of my life?", I ask myself.

At that point something shifts for me, and I know that something must change.

Who this book is for

This book is for anyone looking to re-evaluate or improve their intimate relationship. It will help you to consider the place of your relationship in your life as a whole and to think about how it's been supporting you up until now or otherwise.

If things have not been working as well as you would like, it will give you steps that you can take to get things back on track. And if things have been going well, it will give you ways of taking things to the next level.

If you are reading this book together with your partner, it will give you diverse ways of understanding what has been happening and what you may decide to reconsider. If communication with your partner is difficult or you've decided to read this book alone, you will better understand the things you can put into place yourself to improve things or to recognise that it may be time to move on.

If you are not in a relationship currently, you will better understand past relationships and the challenges that you've experienced so that you can consider how you can avoid those challenges in the future. There are always lessons waiting for us to learn them, and we have the choice as to whether we are ready to learn those lessons. Sometimes we need to go through a cycle or challenge multiple times before being ready to learn our lesson. Wherever you are on that journey, this book will help you make sense of things and to consider what kind of relationship is really going to serve you, and what it may require from you in terms of how you need to show up to make that relationship possible.

Shouldn't relationships just be 'easy'?

Just another statistic?

Few couples on their wedding day suspect that they might become a statistic in the divorce rates that are currently running at around 50% of first marriages, and even higher for second marriages. In fact, how many of the remaining 50% that 'survive' are happy anyway - rather than putting on an appearance of happiness while struggling away behind closed doors? And then there are people who DON'T even manage to keep their difficulties behind closed doors but are visible for the entire world to see. People may look the other way in discomfort, but the signs are clear that something is not OK.

"That would NEVER happen to us...!", we think as we walk proudly down the aisle on one of the happiest days of our life.

We know on some level that few if any of those OTHER couples walking down the aisle making up those statistics would have considered themselves divorce candidates, we just assume that we're special and that could never happen to us.

"We're just cut from a different cloth from those other people," we think as we assume or hope that this kind of breakdown could never happen to us.

So, if we follow a similar process and don't put in place a different strategy, could there be at least a possibility that we might end up at a similar place?

Cultural factors that lead to MANY people struggling in their relationship

We can often assume that the way we currently live in our culture - what we are familiar with in our day-to-day world - is reflective of how human beings have always lived.

"Things have always looked more or less like they are today", we might think.

But is this true? What if human culture and society looked radically different for most of our human story compared with how it looks today? And what if those differences had a strong bearing on why so many of us seem to be struggling with our relationships in some way?

Before the dawning of "civilisation" relationships may have been VASTLY different

It has been well argued that the point of the agricultural revolution and initiation of private property marked a key shift in the human journey[1]. Around ten thousand years ago we shifted from a world where there was extremely

---

[1] Christopher Ryan and Cacilda Jethá, Sex at Dawn

limited scope for ownership of ANY type, to a world of private property. You can imagine our ancestors going to forage for resources in the same way that they and all their predecessors had always done and being confronted with a primitive barrier making the statement that this is now private property.

In comparing human culture with that of our nearest relatives in the animal kingdom it's argued that how we organised our society and relationships before that point was very likely to be substantially different from how we currently do so.

Think about it this way. For 99% of our human journey, the notion of private property - whether in the realm of land, resources, or relationships - didn't really make sense, then could that have any connection with why relationships now seem so difficult and fraught with issues?

In addition, it may have been that men-together and women-together social ties were much stronger due to the nature of work and activities undertaken. Whether in building, hunting, or fighting men may well have had closer ties, while women would have also naturally gravitated together in mutual support.

We now most commonly live in nuclear families with a unit of mum and dad and the children, and in some cases little close social or family support. The respective support networks that would have been in place in earlier societies are much weaker in the modern world. While we enjoy many benefits in terms of comfort, health and wellbeing that are reflected in greater life expectancy for many, there are other natural consequences in these major changes to the form of society.

Post-industrial societies offer many solutions, and some new problems?

Even a few generations ago, the world of work looked vastly different from how it looks today. If you consider the type of work your grandparents or great-grandparents were doing, it was likely to be quite different from the types of work most people are engaged in today. At that time most of the work was on farms, in factories, warehouses, down the pit, at the docks or something similar.

As many of these industries have reduced in scope - at least in terms of the level of labour that is required in them (and certainly in developed countries), many of us have much less access to a same-sex support network that may have been important in sustaining us in the past. In the absence of such support networks, many people find themselves more isolated and potentially reverting back to their partners for support rather than a wider network of friends or colleagues.

Again, have these changes been fully understood and mitigated in terms of the impact on our mental health and on our relationships? If we haven't, should we be really surprised that they have a negative impact on those relationships?

Our Genes are not necessarily on our side.

We arrive with a genetic heritage that was passed onto from our parents and every previous ancestor that has walked the earth. We've come a long way!

When you consider your genetic makeup, and what it is primed to achieve - what is the number one goal of those genes and what are they directing us to achieve through this short space of time that we have in this world?

Are our genes really interested in whether we are happy, have a meaningful life and great relationships? Or do they have another purpose in mind?

As many children, with as many partners as possible?

To perpetuate the species, the number one goal of our genes is to pass themselves on in as many ways as possible. In this sense, we are remarkably like our relatives in the animal kingdom and the reward centres of the brain are wired to move us towards specific types of behaviour and reactions in pursuit of that goal.

And supporting great relationships?

So, if we were just to follow our instincts or urges to have these multiple partners and as many children as we could physically manage, does this sound like a recipe for a positive and meaningful relationship? Or is it possible that in pursuing that kind of behaviour that we are in a sense naturally wired for, that we could cause some problems for ourselves and the people around us?

A helping hand?

Serotonin is a chemical that helps to regulate our mood and helps us to stabilise mood, to regulate anxiety and to experience happiness.[2] Serotonin has several functions in the body and is produced within the gut. The times when you feel positive, secure, and happy are likely to correlate to having healthy levels of serotonin within your body.

When we meet a new partner, we may have several goals and ideas in mind - both consciously and unconsciously. However, after considering what our primal or genetic motivation is, could it be that our genes are rubbing their metaphorical hands at this point that an opportunity might be approaching to make a dent in the genetic makeup of future generations?

---

[2] https://www.healthline.com/health/mental-health/serotonin#serotonin-syndrome

So, amid meeting that new partner, our bodies trigger a DROP in the level of serotonin in our body when we are away from that person... **just in case** we were considering relaxing and taking it easy. No, our genes are saying, there is work to be done here and time is of the essence!

This is why we experience this feeling of anxiety or even panic when we are away from our partner - it is our genes' way of pushing us back to that person.

Missing the red flags?

As we experience this anxiety or need to get back to our new partner or potential mate, is it possible that we could miss some red flags in their behaviour that we might have otherwise objectively been well advised NOT to overlook?

So, it's worth considering whether the goals of our genes and our unconscious behaviours are really aligned with our conscious relationship goals and the type of relationship that we may believe is really going to serve us and our families. If we are just 'going with the flow' and not sufficiently aware of these challenges and paradoxes, could we run into some internal (and external) conflicts?

Re-thinking cultural factors

Sometimes we can be so close to something that it's hard to really evaluate or consider. Like the water that the fish is swimming in, can the fish really look at the water or is it just a given part of the environment in which it swims?

The water that we swim in can be thought of as the culture and environment in which we live which includes things like our media, formal education, family structures and political system. For most of the time we take this for granted as "just the way things are". Like the fish itself swimming around, not really considering whether it likes the water much or would rather change it or be somewhere else!

It's only when we get a shock to that system that we stop to think. We've always trusted the police then we learn that a police officer has been raping or framing the people they were meant to be protecting over many years. Or that we've always put our faith in the church then find that some abuse has been committed, and maybe even covered up over decades by the powers that be. Or that we always loved that "super funny and engaging" guy that we grew up watching on TV, then came face to face with some uncomfortable facts backed up by hundreds of witnesses.

It can be uncomfortable, though at these points we've also got an opportunity to come to a deeper understanding and to progress in some way. Maybe it prompts us to challenge the status quo and to do something quite different. While many people continue to choose to look the other way, aren't we better off when we find the courage to really look at what is happening and be ready to at least consider some alternatives?

So, let's consider what our culture has to say around relationships, and how might this be affecting the stories that we are telling ourselves. Think about whether these assumptions are correct ones likely to lead to great outcomes. Could any of these stories be contributing to you being stuck in a cycle in which you currently find yourself?

"We've got to stay together for the kids".

One idea that may have been implanted in our minds long ago, is that it's always better to stay together for the kids. That by sticking it out in our relationship - which let's say, may not be going as well as we'd like - the kids will be better served and that they'll at least have the stability of being with both parents. We might think that there is some magical factor that means that two parents together with the kids simply guarantees domestic bliss and great outcome for everyone involved. Just like it did for Fred and Rose West maybe, loyal to the end!

"I shouldn't be selfish and just think of me," we might tell ourselves that we should put the kids first and just accept our own misery for their benefit.

Is it true that the kids' best interests are always served by two parents staying together unhappily with a sense of sacrifice for the benefit of children. With this mindset are you likely to show up as effective parents, encouraging your children to pursue their dreams while you yourselves are stuck and refusing yourself the possibility of pursuing your dream of happiness?

It may well be that the relationship can be improved, like countless numbers of our clients telling their stories in videos or online of how through working together to rethink their relationship and put effective strategies into place that they can experience a substantial and meaningful improvement.

In this sense, we can still be an inspiring role model to our children of how we own our challenges and work together to improve them, even after struggling for many years.

But what if we are stuck, and despite our best efforts there is still a gap between our expectations or level of commitment to improve the relationship?

"When we get married THEN it will be happy ever after".

How many famous films convey the dream of marriage, how we find our soulmate then go sailing off into the horizon to live a perfect life? Or that as we see our sweetheart coming down the aisle that our heart melts and that everything just works perfectly from that moment onwards. Sure, we can disagree from time to time and have our challenges, but everything works out in the end if we just hold on to that vision.

Even though we may vaguely know the statistics around divorce, we never think that could be our fate. As noted earlier, it's well known that many marriages end in divorce - in the case of first marriages around 50% according to the statisticians[3].

"That's other people that didn't know what they were doing", we might think. But how many people that eventually do get a divorce, started by thinking that just maybe we could end up being one of those statistics later?

Have you ever been at a wedding where there is some significant conflict like a big row between the bride and groom, or bride and mother-in-law? Maybe it was out in the open or you just sensed this simmering conflict under the surface being contained like a shaky dam holding back a powerful river. Were you wincing wondering how much they had spent on the big day and for how long were they going to hold this show together?

3

https://www.ons.gov.uk/peoplepopulationandcommunity/births deathsandmarriages/divorce/bulletins/divorcesinenglandandw ales/2021https://www.ons.gov.uk/peoplepopulationandcommu nity/birthsdeathsandmarriages/divorce/bulletins/divorcesinengl andandwales/2021

Ironically, some of our clients have shared stories where they believed that serious issues in the relationship before they got married would disappear once they brought the magic of matrimony into the equation. Is this reasonable, or are we then asking too much of marriage if we think that suddenly everything would work like clockwork once we've walked together down the aisle and that we've got a photobook and piece of paper to prove it?

"For love to be real it should be unconditional".

The ideal of unconditional love is often held up as the goal of what we are trying to create or experience through our intimate relationship. It's a lofty ideal and is often presented with a spiritual or timeless quality.

In fact, for people with a religious or spiritual outlook, the sense of being accepted unconditionally by a god or higher power can be inspiring and transformational. Wow, we might think, can I really be acceptable to a god despite my limitations, drawbacks, and mistakes?

While this goal might be meaningful in a religious or spiritual context, how reasonable a goal is it in the arena of our human relationships?

Considering a newborn baby, would it be a good idea to love and protect that baby under all circumstances? Is it possible to spoil the baby for example by being too affectionate? Up until the 1950s psychologists warned parents not to spoil children too much by over tending them[4].

"Let him cry a little more", parents would justify. "It'll do him good and toughen him up."

Some of us today may still be carrying a legacy from being raised under this principle and mindset. The advice has since evolved in recognising what happens when we leave the cries for help or pleas of support from a baby ignored. What message are we giving to the baby by leaving their needs and cries unanswered, and what beliefs could that cultivate in the child as they grow? The baby is powerless to meet their needs so it's arguably our role as parents to support them to the best of our ability during this phase of their life.

A baby surely doesn't need to behave in a certain way, or to contribute in any way to be worthy of being supported in that way. They can make as much mess and smell as they choose and we as parents or caregivers are there for the baby! In that sense the principle of unconditionality DOES indeed make sense in terms of our engagement with a baby.

---

[4] Cupid's Poisoned Arrow by Marnia Robinson

How about in our intimate relationships? Is it true that our partner can behave in ANY way like the baby and expect our attitude or love towards them to remain unchanged? It is helpful to imagine that however unreasonable our partner's behaviour might be, that we are bound by a need to accept and condone that UNCONDITIONALLY, no matter what?

For most people therefore the goal of unconditional love in our intimate relationship is an unrealistic one at best, and a dangerous one at worst. What kind of nonsense might we be ready to go along with if we try to apply this principle to our marriage or relationship? And how careless might our own behaviour become if we feel that we are entitled to expect unconditional love in return?

"If we don't get divorced then that means that everything is ok".

Even with the high rates of divorce mentioned earlier, there can still be a substantial stigma to the idea of getting a divorce. We might think that it represents the ultimate failure. Religion may also play into this belief that because we made this commitment before God and that we were asking for God's support in making the marriage work, that to admit failure would be also undermining God's power in some way. Or God may even come to judge us as being a failure or unworthy in bringing shame upon ourselves and letting Him down.

We may think that any degree of discomfort or pain in the relationship is less painful than the admission to ourselves and the people around us that we've given up on the relationship.

With this idea in our culture, how many of the marriages that survive the statistics we mentioned earlier are happy, rewarding, and functional rather than just surviving or "white knuckling".

"That's not an option for us... Ever!", says the fictional Queen to Prince Philip in The Crown with reference to divorce. But how often does this sentiment take off the table the idea that we could ever consider separating and that we've got to stick it out whatever?

"Getting help is a sign of failure".

If we consider that we should "just know" how to do something, then asking for help can be an uncomfortable admission of failure. Our identity or sense of self may not survive intact when confronted with evidence contrary to the idea that we would be able to fix things ourselves.

"We're grown-ups and we should be able to make relationships work", we might think.

It's interesting that for most of us if our car breaks down by the side of the motorway that we don't have much resistance to the idea that we may need some expert assistance to help us resolve the issue. Maybe it's a blown tyre and we want to change it ourselves, but in most cases we just sense that this is more than we can manage ourselves. We happily get our phone out and call for assistance.

So far, so good.

But why is it that in the case of relationships that we resist the idea that we might need some expert assistance to fix things. And which is a more complex entity in any case, a car, or a human relationship? Which has more moving parts?

"Everyone has a perfect relationship on social media".

We know that people sometimes struggle in relationships, but how much of this do we see on social media? Are people likely to want to open their relationship challenges to the world, or would they rather keep their dirty linen in private?

At times that we ourselves may be struggling with our relationship, it can be dispiriting to open our social media feed to see nothing but shiny happy people living the dream, sipping cocktails on some tropical beach with a lineup of happy, well-behaved kids in tow! How easy is it to think about the reality of our own challenges at that point and to think there is something wrong with us?

If everyone else is just showing their best moments, do we really want to be real and share the reality of our own challenges?

"Relationships are never perfect".

"Everyone has arguments", we might say. "It's normal."

If we think that all relationships are challenging, it can cause us to lower our ambitions of how good a relationship can even be. It's like we give up before we even begin.

"Yes, we're having a miserable relationship," we reassure ourselves. "Just like everyone else."

Is this true, and how would we know in any case? Is there something about relationships that makes them automatically difficult, or could there be something that we are doing that is somehow contributing to those difficulties? Are we willing to accept our current challenges or are we open to the possibility that a better way of relating is available if we are willing to act?

What do we learn at school?

If the messaging we receive as adults around relationships from our culture can be mixed, how about what we learn through the education system as children? Based on OECD data, average teaching hours for 14–15-year-old pupils in England are 26.8 per week[5]. This means that over the 39 weeks of school per year, and the eleven years of compulsory education, that even allowing for some time off due to sickness a student can expect to receive **over eleven thousand hours** of classroom tuition over their school life, even before considering homework, self-study, vocational education, additional qualifications, and university.

If we consider that our success in relationships is likely to influence not only our own happiness but that of our children and others around us, how many of those hours are devoted to learning about relationships?

I remember learning some basic reproductive biology about where babies come from - though even then it was limited by the embarrassment of the teacher and the sniggering from the back of the classroom. I also remember as a teenager, one of the teachers tentatively coming in at the beginning of a tutorial to talk about how to put a condom on - thinking about the "ambiance" in the class, I'd be open to the suggestion that teachers should be better rewarded for their efforts!

In any case, it's safe to say that these educational experiences were a very small fraction of my eleven

---

5

https://assets.publishing.service.gov.uk/government/upl oads/system/uploads/attachment_data/file/1031290/Rev iew_of_time_in_school_and_16_to_19_settings.pdf thousand hours and didn't leave me much the wiser in terms of how to create and develop successful intimate relationships.

So where do we learn our relationship skills?

Even though what we learn at school about relationships may be limited, there is somewhere that we do learn a lot... and it's not in a classroom environment.

We come into the world as little sponges, and we learn a huge amount in the first years of our life through observation and modelling. As young children we are not able to objectively analyse and consider what we see in the world around us, but we internalise it and consider that it's just the way things are.

Rather than deliberately and consciously choosing which ideas and behaviours we like (and what to retain) and those that we don't like, we just internalise them as a given truth or 'this is how relationships are.'

Perhaps by a miracle our parents or caregivers are having the most incredible, blissful, perfect relationship and they are shining role-models of a happy and functional marriage. But just in case they are not, is it possible that we are witnessing and internalising some ideas and behaviours that might give us a similar outcome to the one that we've seen in them as our role models?

Is it reasonable to continue those behaviours while expecting that we are going to create a different or better outcome than the one we have witnessed?

Sometimes we may even CONSCIOUSLY recognise that something unhealthy is going on, and we might say to ourselves (or even out loud to someone else), that this isn't right. We could see that what we are witnessing doesn't look any good, and that we would NEVER be that person reacting in this way or behaving in such a damaging manner.

The irony here is that repeatedly, even with a conscious recognition that we reject a certain approach or behaviour there is a substantial chance of us repeating a similar pattern ourselves in any case.

Relationships pay dividends WHEN they work.

What clearer barometer of our overall well-being than the well-functioning or otherwise of our relationships, and especially the relationship with our intimate partner? With our work with couples, we have the privilege of engaging with couples every day where they are encountering substantial challenges that have got them to a point of no return.

"Either we sort this now, or it could be the end of our relationship", they often say when they first reach out.

On the flipside, what about when our relationships are healthy and stable, and we can create real magic, or a 'masterpiece' as we sometimes say. One of the models we use helps us to identify what a CREATIVE relationship looks like. So, what does this mean?

Love Never Dies

How we show up in our lives affects the people around us. We 'ripple into the lives of the people we meet'[6], whether it's friends, colleagues or just people we meet in day-to-day life. Being around someone who is really struggling emotionally, it's very difficult not to be affected by that.

You have observed when someone has lost their cool with someone in a shop or in the street? You've been with a friend or on a date and they've reacted in a way that shocked you or went against your values - like they gave the waiter a dressing down for bringing the wrong meal.

What feeling did that leave you with?

How much more important how we show up in our relationship! Rather than a fleeting interaction we weave

---

[6] A Matter of Death and Life by Irv & Marilyn Yalom

26

our lives together with our partner, and the fabric or quality of that impact is felt not only by us but the people we interact with. If we share 3 meals per day over a 50-year relationship that would be more than fifty thousand meals! There are likely to be times when we are apart, but even if the true figure were a fraction of this - it's still a lot of time to interact!

When we show up in a positive state, it can be uplifting for everyone around. They then carry something of this energy into their day and into their lives, sometimes consciously or otherwise unconsciously. As they go on to interact with others, they retain an imprint of those previous interactions. In that sense we can say that the energy we put out resonates around the world and never disappears. If we choose to put love out into the world it never dies but continues to flow into people's lives and relationships even after we are gone.

The Magic of the Dance!

Have you ever seen a couple - of whatever gender combination - dancing beautifully together? When the dynamic is right between the partners and they are both really tuned into the music, something can be created that is beyond words. It stops us in our tracks and is compelling. In that flow and harmony something is created that can touch us deeply, in a way that simply walking from A to B cannot. What feeling does that evoke in you?

A solo dance can also be beautifully performed but it may be that we feel that the dance of our life cannot be complete without sharing the dance with a partner. If so, we need to not only learn some dance steps, to choose the right music, to practise and to also identify ways that the dance could break down if we don't approach it in the right way. Otherwise, we may be left hoping that by chance the dance is going to work perfectly!

The dance is a theme that we will come back to later and is a useful analogy of the relationship in so many ways. Just like our relationship the dance can be anywhere on a scale from a complete disaster to something so beautiful that it moves us to tears and uplifts our life and the lives of those around us. Also, that just as our life doesn't tend to be perfectly choreographed, the dance can take us in unexpected and creative directions.

One plus one CAN be more than two!

Each one of us in the relationship brings certain gifts and strengths to the table. We have different perspectives and life experiences that can feed into the relationship. Let's say one of us is practical and great at problem solving, while the other is more emotionally aware and perceptive around relationships and feelings. Could we have the possibility of COMPLEMENTING each other so that we are more and better together than each of us would be alone?

Another common example would be where one of us is naturally very nurturing and loves looking after young children, whereas the other is more comfortable in a work environment and contributes financially and supports the family in other ways. What does it take for us to be able to play to our strengths and again to create something TOGETHER that would be potentially more difficult to create on our own?

Even amid our struggles it's useful to remember that this synergy is at least a possibility, even though it may feel like a long way from our current reality.

Our lives are intertwined.

In their book A Matter of Death and Life, Irv and Marilyn Yalom share the journey of her cancer diagnosis and death and his process of making sense of her death and their sixty year plus relationship. They had met at a dance when teenagers, married, had four children, worked together as well as living in several countries and travelling widely for more than half a century.

In one section, Irv shares how even with Marilyn's terminal cancer diagnosis that there are memories and stories from their life that she has better recollection of compared to his own. In re-reading the books he had authored; he finds stories and anecdotes that he struggles to identify or visualise, and he is sure that she would have clearly remembered certain contexts that he could no longer access.

That in some respects she is carrying the memory of his life, as it's only through their discussion that he can come to remember important events that they have experienced together. And recognising that with her approaching death, that aspects of his life will be lost forever once Marilyn dies.

After her death, he has a sense that even day to day activities like watching TV are not fully real until he has shared it with his wife, which he is now unable to do. That his life has lost some richness or meaning through her death.

These are poignant examples of how close we can feel to our partner, and how in some respects that our lives become one and intertwined. We can still have separate interests and activities of course, though it may be that in the sharing of those activities that we feel fulfilled and complete.

A core part of the human experience

We are born into a relationship with our caregivers, and babies only identify a sense of themselves at the age of approximately six months. Until then we understand the world purely in relation to our caregivers and consider ourselves as part of them. Whether we are the first child to arrive, or whether we are born into an environment where other children are already present, relationships shape and define us in important ways even before we leave the house to make relationships further afield.

When we encounter others outside of our immediate family, the relationships that we form and the way we relate to others is a powerful contributor to our experience of ourselves and the world around us. Maybe we experience some disappointment or even betrayal, or we learn that certain behaviour gives us a sense of power or control that makes us feel better.

Whatever relationship dynamics we experience, the lessons we learn play a key role in shaping us into who we are.

Our natural state is in relationship.

When thinking about our relationships, could there be any parallels or lessons to be taken from the world of physics reflecting the nature of matter? Is it more helpful to consider elements in isolation or in terms of the relationships between those elements?

The smallest component of matter is an atom, but what is an atom? In addition to a nucleus, atoms are composed of protons with a positive electrical charge and electrons with a negative charge. If the number of protons and electrons are equal, then the atom is electronically neutral[7]. So even at the smallest

---

[7] https://en.wikipedia.org/wiki/Atom

component level we can say that atoms or matter are characterised by elements in relation to one another held together or split apart by the relationship of forces between them.

So, if all matter is composed of atoms, maybe we ourselves follow a similar pattern of living in relationship to others, always affected in some way by the nature and functioning of those relationships between component parts - the relationships between people. Could the forces of our relationships and what holds us together or leads us apart resemble the forces that play out at an atomic level?

A legacy for our children

Often when clients are telling us why this work is so important and meaningful to them, they describe the impact that their relationship has on their children - either on existing children or the anticipated impact on any future children that they want to have.

"I wouldn't want to bring our children into this environment", people might say and in fact delay or avoid having children altogether believing the potential impact to outweigh any positive expectation that they might have.

"I just know that the kids pick up on the tension between us", we might think as we wonder how that tension could lead to stress and impacts in other ways such as their ability to concentrate and function at school.

Having considered that so much of what we learn about relationships comes from the environment into which we are born, it's helpful to think about what kind of "relationship education legacy" we'd like to leave for our children. When they look back at their childhood and think about how it shaped their lives, including in their relationships, what kind of story would we like them to tell?

Also, even if you've had difficulties, is it too late to change the narrative and to show that change is possible? Could it be that the contrast between the difficulties that you've experienced in the past, and a subsequent more functional relationship could be the most inspiring example of all?

Even though there are messages in our culture that say we should "stay together for the children", the research shows that an ongoing failing or toxic relationship is the worst possible outcome for our children[8]. Far better to work to improve things, or in the worst case if that's not a possibility what else might you need to do to ensure a healthy environment for your children?

---

[8] The Seven Principles for Making Marriage Work by John M. Gottman

It's sometimes said that children don't listen much to what their parents SAY, but that they never fail to follow the example or model of what they DO! So how is your relationship affecting your children and what would it mean for them to them to see you step up and take responsibility to make a change?

When we choose to stay stuck

Sometimes even with a sense that something better could be possible, we decide not to go on that journey but to stay stuck. It's like we sense that the change is going to ask questions of us that we are simply not ready to answer. Maybe we are so attached to an idea or an identity that it would be more painful to question or give up that idea than it would be to go on enduring the pain we are experiencing.

"Hang on," we think. "If I give up that idea, then that would lead to having to question other things and all of sudden what else I might need to confront?"

And if we've been struggling with a challenge for a while, holding on and hoping for something to change but not acting it can get harder over time to address it. This is sometimes referred to as the sunk cost fallacy. It's like if we finally do decide to act, we'd not only be admitting that we are wrong, but that through inaction or resistance we've been choosing to continue the struggle needlessly for years. The implications of that decision on ourselves and the people around us is more than we want to confront.

So, we choose to stay stuck.

A prison of our own making

Whether we've ever set foot in a prison, many of us have a clear sense that to give up our freedom in jail would be a big step back and a life-limiting factor. We couldn't go where we choose, associate with who we want to and find ways of expressing our life in a way that is meaningful to us. We would have these very visible things all around us - walls and bars and so on - reminding us that we are in prison.

For most of us we are not in a physical prison, but does that necessarily mean that we are free? What beliefs and decisions are keeping us in a familiar but painful situation where we are not unable, but unwilling to go beyond the boundaries that we have created for ourselves?

It's like a security firm comes to our own house and boards up all the doors and windows, and we happen to be inside at the time[9]. Sometimes on recognising this we might feel a sense of relief to know that finally we really are safe now.

---

[9] The Untethered Soul by Michael A. Singer

"Sure, we can't go anywhere", we think. "But at least we're not in danger."

Could it be that the things that we rely on to keep us safe also have an effect of limiting our growth and expansion. We could decide to stay in that comfort zone - maybe we arrange some food deliveries - but would there get to a point where staying there limits our ability to live our life to the full?

Empowering you to take back control of your life.

Once we've been looking unsuccessfully for a solution for a while, it's easy to get down on ourselves.

"What's wrong with me?", we might ask. "Why can't I just work this one out?"

Sometimes we might simply give up and put the problem in the "too difficult" category. It can't be done; we might tell ourselves.

One common issue is that if we're trying hard, but focussing on something we just cannot control, we end up feeling down and disempowered. Like on the day of our parade with the rain pelting down, we look out of the window with our summer clothes prepared and we scream internally at the unfairness of the world, and why things never work out for me. How does it make us feel if we get involved in judging or trying to control something that is outside of our remit, like the weather? How much further forward does this take us?

Similarly in relationships, we can get stuck (and even depressed) when we spend time and energy getting involved in things that are simply outside of our control.

"She should be more focussed on working on the relationship," we might say or internally think. "She's too focussed on work." While making a request or invitation to our partner is one thing, when that flips into making demands of what our partner SHOULD do, how does that make us feel? One of the most important steps that you can take is to recognise that your energy is going to be best spent focussing on things that you can do something about.

When our ideas simply do not stack up any more

Have you ever come to realise that a long-held belief that you have bought into is simply unsustainable and doesn't make any sense? Maybe you'd bought into a belief that immigrants are lazy and have just come here to take welfare payments. Then at some point you met an immigrant family who are not only friendly but hard working. Or you recognise that your own family had arrived with little a couple of generations ago with nothing and raised themselves up through commitment and sacrifice.

Perhaps you've been holding onto that flawed idea for a while, with a sinking sense that you've missed something, or otherwise that understanding can come suddenly. These foundational beliefs that have been guiding us but that we come to realise do not line up with the reality of the world around us have been described as 'false premises' [10].

An important aspect of this book is going to be to reconsider those false premises that we hold - especially around the areas of relationships. What ideas could we have been buying into on some level that could have been holding us back or keeping us feeling trapped and unhappy? Imagine how our life could change now we are ready to stand back and reevaluate those false premises.

As toddlers we have a lot to learn!

Imagine a young toddler could hold a belief that, "I'm allowed to have as much ice cream as I want!". That is simply his understanding of the world at this point based on how much he loves ice cream and what an important thing it is for him. Surely if you like something so much, and now you know the word for that tasty thing you've

---

[10] The Vortex by Esther Hicks

been given, you just say that word as it continues to appear, right?

But what might happen when this toddler encounters a parent that one day says, "We're having dinner soon, so that's enough ice cream for now."

At this point the toddler is confronted with an issue that the world is apparently not conforming to the belief - or "false premise" - that he has understood to govern his world. And there's at least a possibility that there could be an emotional reaction to this perceived outrage. There could even be a meltdown!

At this stage, he could resist and hold on insisting to himself that this was some kind of misunderstanding or temporary glitch, and that the world will return to its correct order soon enough. "Dad was just having a bad day", he might think.

And for as long as the idea is held onto that "I can have as much ice cream as I want", it's likely that the same reaction could be repeated day after day. And we tend to be more tolerant or forgiving of this kind of behaviour in young children, or even see it as endearing and part of a journey that we all travel!

We can also be toddler-like!

Maybe you can think of ideas from later in your life that you have come to re-evaluate in this way. Something

39

that you believed with certainty even during your adolescence or early adulthood that has been challenged enough by your experience that you have been ready to admit to yourself, "Hey, maybe I was getting it a bit wrong there!"

Suppose you had this idea that all vegans were sandal wearing hippies, then you found out that your favourite sports person is a vegan. How can that be, we initially ask ourselves as we come to terms with this world beating sporting hero hasn't been eating any of the red meat that we've always told ourselves is so essential for high performance.

At these stages we're presented with an opportunity to reevaluate our false premises and come to a deeper understanding that better accords with the reality of the world we live in. If we choose to take that opportunity, we have the chance to upgrade our ideas, refresh our software and eliminate at least some of the times when we become aware of the gap. And as in the case of the toddler who eventually must concede, "Ok, maybe mummy and daddy really DO control the ice cream", how does our relationship with the world around us change when we review and correct our false premises? What different emotions are we likely to be aware of with our corrected understanding?

Uncertainty can disappear in the presence of new evidence.

Imagine that you are sitting by a river enjoying the day with a friend. The river is wide enough at the point you are enjoying, and you are debating together whether it's possible for someone to jump across that gap to the bank on the other side.

"Yeah, I would say it could be possible," one of you says.

"No way, it's simply can't be done", says the other.

After you've been debating for a while, a third person enters the picture and as you both watch on, jumps across that gap landing safely on the other side. At this point, the debate becomes redundant. It's not even about who was right or wrong - you were speculating and those were your opinions before seeing what you just witnessed but now there is no debate to be had.

The only issue is if someone claims to have been looking the other way and denies what you have seen. This can be us when we simply don't want to recognise a new reality. It's not that we don't KNOW the truth, more that we don't want to know.

The costs of holding onto our delusion

For as long as we stubbornly hold onto ideas that no longer make any sense, there's a good chance that we'll engage in extreme or dysfunctional behaviour to enable us to maintain the myth at least to ourselves. Like when we believe ourselves to be the rightful election winner, but the actual results based on the evidence go against us. What insanity might we unleash in a vain attempt to avoid having to accept that reality?

The comedian and actor Kevin Hart[11] shared an example from his childhood when his father had decided to take on his brother in a basketball head-to-head. You might be younger and fitter, his father had thought, but that's ok I can still show you how to play. In fact, Kevin's brother comfortably won the game, but his father wasn't about to accept the reality of defeat. According to his story, a few minutes later his father returned and set his dog on the two boys that had to scramble up a fence to get away from the attacking dog, as his father laughed on from the sidelines!

What are we ready to do to perpetuate a delusional belief? Think about the impact on the people around us when we doggedly hold onto an idea that doesn't make any sense any more in relation to the facts. What would it take for us to be ready to accept that we got it wrong, and that we can progress in a healthy and reasonable way?

---

[11] I Can't Make this Up: Life Lessons by Kevin Hart

Our relationship-focussed 'false premises'

By the time you reach the end of this book you will have examined and re-evaluated a number of these misunderstandings or 'false premises' that are affecting your relationship now and preventing you from creating a relationship that serves you and the people around you. In some cases that will enable you to come into better alignment with the status quo, such as in the ice cream example. In others, it may be that as you correct these misunderstandings that there will be some external changes that we need to instigate to our relationships as we take these into account.

On the other hand, if our goal is to stubbornly hold onto our existing ideas that haven't been serving us, we may have limited results like in the cases above. We might even unleash even more pain on ourselves or the people around us in a desperate attempt to cling on. In those cases, we tend to simply look for information that confirms an existing belief, leading us to keep going around in circles.

The importance of clarity

What does it mean to have clarity about our situation, and what does it look like when we don't?

Problems versus SYMPTOMS of problems

If our house has a problem in the foundations, we could live in that building for some time without being aware that we have any problem. Let's call this stage 1, where we're blissfully unaware that anything is amiss. The problem is unseen and it's not causing us any functional problem at this stage at all.

We then eventually move on to Stage 2 when something happens - maybe it's some particularly heavy rainfall - and a symptom arises of the problem that was already there. Let's say that this is a crack in the wall of our house that appears overnight. At this point we say to ourselves "Ok, now we have a problem", though as we described this is not completely true as technically you ALREADY had a problem in stage 1. The issue was that you couldn't SEE the problem at that point.

Then we move into Stage 3 where we need to deal with the problem, though the way we deal with it is normally through treating the SYMPTOM of the problem rather than the underlying issue. Unless we happen to be a builder, this tends to lead to a trip to the DIY store returning with polyfiller and either some paint or a roll of wallpaper.

"I've got this one," we say, and we get busy filling in the crack as best we can and making it look a bit better with the help of our trusty wallpaper.

"Job done", we say, though even at that stage it may also be difficult to avoid that creeping feeling that this may not be the end of the story.

Sure enough in Stage 4, another problem arises which might be another crack, or the return of the previous crack, or it's a completely different issue like a leak from a split pipe. We go back to work with our wallpaper but before long it's difficult to pretend anymore that things are ok and eventually, we might start to wonder about the viability of this whole DIY approach.

It's worth remembering that there is often no shortage of effort during this phase. We could be spending a lot of time and energy re-filling, patching, and lining up that wallpaper in a futile attempt to cover up the problem. This can make it even more demoralising when we see that wallpaper under rubble in the next phase.

Stage 4 usually culminates in a problem so big that we just cannot avoid the truth anymore. Maybe a whole wall falls, and we're faced with the truth that we need a fundamental rethink to our approach. At this point, we may abandon the project altogether and find somewhere else to live.

"Hmmm, I do like fresh air," we think. "But I'm not sure that we can live here without a wall on one side of the building."

At this point we may "abandon ship" and decide the building is simply not viable anymore. We simply move out and look for somewhere else to live. If we run into problems with the new place, we might move on again and continue the cycle.

Or we move into Stage 5 when we decide to get professional help to identify and resolve the actual problem - normally with the help of a builder or other professional. If we're honest we know that while we can have a good attempt at wallpapering, we're not likely to dig up the floor to investigate or remedy at a deeper level - we just don't have the skillset. We're committed to this building, and we recognise that for it to be really viable requires a more fundamental approach compared to the quick fixes that we've been trying to apply.

Once the underlying problem has been rectified - perhaps by underpinning the building - everything we re-build in Stage 6 has a fundamentally different quality than everything that preceded it. At this point, we can invest with confidence knowing that the foundations are solid and that we can put the wallpaper into storage. We may decide to use wallpaper to beautify our house, but we will no longer need it to cover up problems for which wallpaper is simply unable to resolve. And now we can consider adding to the property with an extension or additional storey, which in the case of our relationship might be to get engaged or to have a baby.

This process of identifying and dealing with the underlying problem, is a way of understanding what we mean by clarity. It may well be that a few well targeted actions to resolve those fundamental issues could give us a hugely different outcome, but we are not able to take those actions without a correct initial diagnosis.

Until we reach that correct diagnosis there is a good chance that we'll just be coping with our problems (like the wallpaper), while getting into a cycle of despair and disappointment as we encounter issue after issue. Imagine how difficult it would be to follow the wallpapering approach without starting to feel some despair or frustration before long, even thinking that the problem is simply not resolvable.

Coping in your relationship versus getting to the root cause

Using the analogy above, how have the cracks appeared in your relationship? What have been your coping mechanisms or strategies of dealing with things (like the wallpaper)? Has that ever become like a cycle where the crack reappears telling you that the things that you've been doing haven't addressed the underlying issues? What has been the cost of that on yourself and the relationship?

We've chosen our partner in the past, but are we still choosing them?

One of the goals of this book is to help you to understand whether your relationship is viable and what it would take to make it work at a level where you can both thrive, rather than just to survive. So why is it important to consider whether and how we are choosing our partner day by day, rather than having a sense that we choose our partner "at some point in the past"[12]?

When we get lazy

It can be easy to think that once we've landed our partner that its job done and that things will just work from that point. We let ourselves go and fail to sustain our efforts either for ourselves or towards our partner. If you take physical fitness as a parallel, what happens to us when we don't maintain those habits to keep ourselves in good shape?

In our marriage or relationship, we may find ourselves behaving in ways that we would never have considered at the start of the relationship, or in ways that we would never behave towards a new or potential partner. What is it about our partner that makes us think that they should accept a lower standard of attention or love compared to what we would give to someone else? How could a feeling of inattention or being taken for granted

---

[12] The Practice of Love, Lair Torrent

impact on the level of connection that you feel in your relationship, and what could be the cost of this over time?

We choose each other every day.

What if every day we spent with our partner was an active and deliberate choice to be with that person, to share our lives together? Ultimately, is it not the case that if we so decided we could each be living entirely different lives?

"No, you don't understand that we've got an agreement," you might say. "It's called a marriage certificate and neither of us is going anywhere!"

Is our vision for our relationship some kind of restrictive contract where we've signed over our freedom to someone for the rest of our life? If we agree to live in a state of captivity with that person where we can't exercise our personal choice anymore, then it's worth considering what level of connection we are likely to develop in such a deal.

In addition, it could be true that a written or unwritten agreement may well be in place at the current time regarding our commitment to each other. And, that there are other kinds of agreement to which we have access if we choose which could supersede the current agreement? In the case of our marriage, it's a familiar one that begins with a "D".

So, what if rather than taking our partner and relationship as a given, we could show up in a way that honours our personal choices. We have freely chosen to be together now, and we continue to make that decision for as long as it's the right decision for both of us. How could adopting this level of attentiveness and focus transform the way that we show up in the relationship and the outcomes that we are likely to experience?

Time on our side?

Maybe we've known for a while that we are unhappy in our marriage or relationship but that addressing it has seemed too complicated or difficult. Set alongside the varied challenges that we are navigating; our relationship just seems like one thing too many. We might also think that there will be time later to address this and that we'll naturally and suddenly arrive at that time.

"That," we might say to ourselves, "will be the moment that I eventually get around to dealing with this discomfort. For now, we'll just make the best of it."

Costs inflicted on other areas of our life.

Could it be that the time we spend like this in the waiting room causes negative effects in other areas of our life? By deciding not to address our relationship struggles, do we go on to struggle in things which could have otherwise worked much better, and provided greater satisfaction?

Perhaps our mood affects the way we interact with our children or other family members so that rather than supporting a needy child, we react in a more impatient or reactive way. What are we then conveying to that child in terms of being willing to stand up and ask for what they need. What memories are we implanting through the message that we are sending at their moment of need and how could that affect our relationship with them in the future?

Or maybe we are affected at work by being less resilient or flexible than we might otherwise be. Do we sometimes stop in the middle of a task and think to ourselves about an unresolved argument that we had, or wondering how we are going to tell our partner about something that we know is going to upset them. Might our colleagues hold back from engaging with us as they see that we are struggling, and they don't know how to react? Can you think of anyone like this where we don't perhaps know exactly what the problem is, but that we sense something isn't right? That person who you feel is a shell of themselves, or even the "walking dead".

Are we granted another day?

It's generally understood - at least logically - that while we are alive today that one day in the not-too-distant future this will no longer be the case! Even though death is often a taboo subject in our culture, don't we recognise on some level this precious window of life that we are currently experiencing? We know the stories of familiar faces - family members or friends, or celebrities or film stars - that we've felt a connection with that now rest in cemeteries or memorial gardens around the world.

The question is whether we've understood the transitory nature of life enough to really know that today could be our last. Like countless others before us, we could have "rosy cheeks in the morning and be white bones by the evening."[13] In fact, we don't know when we will breathe our last breath - whether through an accident or an illness or through the effects of ageing on the body and mind. It's like death walks alongside us from the moment we are born, waiting for the right moment to make an introduction and to finally shake our hand.

We know surely that this introduction is coming but do we really KNOW deep down? How would our life be lived differently, and what greater urgency and focus could we summon? What if we really internalised this understanding that we don't know how long we've got left to sing the song of our life? Would we approach our challenges differently, and would we be less willing to just sit and wait and along our unresolved challenges to go on and on, dragging us down every day? Would we

---

[13] Letters by Rennyo Shonin

still put our relationship into the 'too difficult' category if we saw our life draining away like the sand in a timer?

Part 1 - Recognising where we are.

Taking the longer view

How easy is it to get lost in the challenges of the day whether they be in work, dealing with the kids or getting done any number of tasks on our to-do list? Many of us are busy spinning multiple plates and it can be difficult to stand back and see things in a bigger context. We then struggle to make sense of things and can even wonder what's the point, or to eventually give up. What if we could periodically step back and review where we are in our relationship and in life in the context of a bigger journey.

Our relationship in the context of our life

We came into this world in a certain context, with gifts and resources and surrounded by others. Whatever challenges were playing out when we arrived in the world, it's likely that compared to many other humans - both now and in the past - we were presented with many gifts and opportunities even from the start.

It's also possible that we weren't fully developed and mature from the outset - we had lessons to be learnt along the journey, which had to be learnt if we were going to realise our potential. From obvious things like learning to walk and talk, to the way we dealt with others there were likely some relationship lessons to be better understood.

If you think back to the relationships that you had during your childhood with your friends and family, and moving forward to your first romantic relationships, there are probably things that you've come to re-think over that time. Perhaps you even look back in shock or amusement at the way you've conducted yourself in the past!

In any case, it's useful to consider that this learning journey is an ongoing process and that there's at least a possibility that there are some lessons - big and small - that are still to be learnt in the future. The question is whether we are open to learning those lessons as we continue to develop and improve or whether we prefer to stay stuck in our current state.

From birth to death

Whatever beliefs you hold about previous or future lives, we can see ourselves on a journey or timeline that stretches back to our birth in the past, and forward to our death in the future. We are somewhere on that journey, though we don't know with any certainty where that journey will end. What we can consider are the types of questions that we might ask ourselves when we come to look back on our lives, and the most familiar challenges people tend to face at that point. What kind of questions might we have about our relationships at that point, and the decisions that we've made?

In her book The Top Five Regrets of the Dying, author Bronnie Ware shares her experience of working with many dying patients in considering the most common questions and regrets that are raised.

The first (and most common) regret is that "I wish I'd had the courage to live a life true to myself, not the life others expected of me." It's worth re-reading that statement and pausing for a moment with some calming breaths to absorb the meaning of it in our context.

There are many elements of the expectations of others in the way that societal values can shape and imprison us, stopping us from being true to ourselves. Are we willing to let other people's expectations stop us from living the life that is meaningful to us? What would be the cost of holding ourselves back in this respect and having to confront the consequences of such a decision?

Grieving the life we never had

In their book A Matter of Death and Life, Irv and Marilyn Yalom consider the prevalence of death anxiety as one of the most common challenges that people bring into therapy. The sense of a life not fully lived is one of the main contributors to this condition, where we come to feel that we haven't fulfilled our potential in some way.

This leads to a sense of anxiety that there were things that needed to be done, that we held ourselves back from and didn't complete.

They consider how our life in relationships plays into this dynamic. They pose the interesting question of whether it's more challenging to grieve the death of a partner when the relationship has been positive and magical, versus the loss of a partner with whom we've had a strained or challenging relationship. Logically we might think that it's more challenging to grieve the loss of a dearly beloved partner, and where the partner dies young or unexpectedly there can be an element of a lost opportunity. What could they have achieved or experienced if they could have lived into old age we might wonder.

With the death of a partner with whom we have had a difficult relationship, the feelings are likely to be more complex. In a sense we might be grieving the partner, feeling that whatever difficulties they experienced or presented that they were still doing their best. It's likely after all that their challenges came from some degree of trauma or unprocessed emotions in their own story, especially during childhood. Although if they themselves were not looking for help to resolve those emotions, any ideas we have remain speculative.

However, there is another element of grief that could be as strong or even stronger. Because in choosing to say yes to a life unhappily surviving with that partner, we have also chosen to say no to a completely different life. We are left wondering what might have been possible had we had the courage to address the situation, and where a different path had been available. There was a fork - or perhaps many forks - in the road with an opportunity to pursue a completely different journey, though for whatever reason we chose not to take those paths. At this stage though we can only wonder what that future might have looked like had we made a different choice, or even what riches may have been waiting for us there.

Death may be a taboo in our culture, and often put into the "too sensitive" category and thus ignored. Don't talk about that, you'll make people feel uncomfortable, we might think. But what could be more important than doing everything we can to prepare for that time of reckoning where we look back and think about the decisions that we've made? Would it be better to confront those challenges now while we still have some life ahead of us, or to wait until we're approaching the finish line with little time to change course or to make up?

We 'ripple into the lives of the people around us...'

Do you know people who are a joy to be around? Those people that fill the room with hope and positivity and where even their challenges and obstacles are like food to feed their inspiration and passion?

How about the opposite scenario? Do you know people where whatever the drama of the day, you walk away feeling heavy and down after interacting with them. Like nothing is good enough for them, and nobody escapes their critical or negative judgements. We go home and wonder why we don't feel like doing anything for the rest of the day, so we put the TV on and channel surf the rest of the day or we crack open a bottle of wine. We're not sure why, but we just don't feel like doing anything else.

Is it possible to cut ourselves off from the influence or emotional state of the people we spend time with? Or more likely are we inevitably going to be affected at least to some extent by the people around us? What kind of person do we want to be, and what implication does that have in terms of our choices of the people that we want to spend time with?

This has been described as how we 'ripple into the lives of the people around us.'[14] So if we take it as a given that the people around us will be affected by our emotional state and our behaviour, what kind of effect would we like to leave them with?

We know on some level that our challenging relationship is one of the factors that puts us into a negative state. After a while, we might not feel like ourselves where we used to be such a happy and energetic person but that

---

[14] Irv Yalom & Marilyn Yalom, A Matter of Death and Life

we've lost that spark along the way. How do other people in our life - like our family and friends - pick up on that, and how might we be impacting on them indirectly by the way we are showing up?

When we settle for less

By leaving a challenging relationship situation unaddressed, who is impacted by that decision? The first answer is that we ourselves are impacted by the draining sense of feeling stuck in a cycle that we can't seem to break. What's wrong with me, we might think as we keep applying the strategies that we know, while continuing to be aware of their limited and diminishing effect.

How about our partner? Is it possible that by continuing the cycle we are also contributing to their challenges? What is the effect on their day-to-day life of the energy that they are spending coping with the stress of things not really working, and the issues that they are not able to express or resolve because the relationship is holding us back in some way?

Is it possible that our children are also affected by the relationship challenges that we are choosing not to address? Do their schoolwork, learning or relationships suffer because of worry or stress about the atmosphere at home and sensing that things are not right in the relationships around them? How are the things they are witnessing going to set a foundation for their future success and happiness, or otherwise? What if we were to see our children struggling with their own difficult relationships in the future, while having to acknowledge that those difficulties have a similar flavour to our own unresolved challenges?

The wider context

If we're not able to resolve our current relationship challenges, would my partner even be happier alone or with someone else? Could it be that there is someone out there - more aligned in values - with whom my partner could be much happier? And how about that potential future partner, dreaming about a life with somebody who would love to build an incredible life with them?

And what about that person who could be a wonderful fit for us, if we really weren't able to shift our current impasse? Who might that person be who would love to build an incredible future, that is unable to do so because we are holding onto something that isn't working because we're not taking action to resolve things? Are we willing to deprive not only ourselves but also that other person of a happy and rewarding life?

How would each of those people then show up in their day to day lives, at work and with family and friends? How many people could be affected by that decision to stay stuck and to not resolve our issues?

You needed this book a long time ago.

Most of the time when people reach out for support with their relationship, it is not the first argument that has triggered that decision to step up. Often things are left to run so that we get caught in a cycle that nobody either recognises or can stop. Then the pattern sets in, and we withdraw or find other ways to cope with a demanding situation.

This section of the book is to help us to understand our starting point so that we can effectively navigate from there. We might be holding a great map in our hands, but if we don't know where we are starting from it could be of limited value.

Gradual deterioration or sudden explosion

It is sometimes said that if the frog is dropped into boiling water he jumps out, whereas when the water is gradually heated up, he slowly gets cooked. Relationships can be like this where there isn't a single trigger but rather a slow and gradual deterioration over time that we might not easily spot. Then we look in the mirror one day and say - like so many clients have shared - that we are no longer the person that we once were. That we are unrecognisable from our younger more vibrant self, with a sense of having been broken by our unresolved issues.

Maybe we've lost our self-confidence, and we no longer want to be around people. Or perhaps we were previously such a happy person but that nothing feels exciting or positive anymore. Rather than looking forward to life with energy and passion we are simply surviving and struggling to make sense of how we got to a point where nothing feels truly rewarding. We might feel a kind of numbness to our core, and even on special occasions we are trying to summon up some joy but all we find is emptiness.

We often see people broken by a situation that they have allowed to deteriorate without realising or understanding the personal costs that they are enduring or the impacts on the people around them. It can be uncomfortable to realise the impact of having let a demanding situation persist, and sometimes we may simply not be ready to accept that.

At the same time, how uncomfortable could it be to know that we had the opportunity to wake up but didn't take that opportunity. Instead, we reverted to the comfortable and sank back into the challenges that we know so well, pretending that the issue either wasn't there, or just an inevitable consequence of being in a relationship?

"Everyone struggles, and no relationship works anyway," we reassure ourselves bleakly.

Something pushed you to wake up.

To be reading this book and to be not only contemplating a different type of relationship, but believing that some kind of change is possible, you must have a vision on some level that change is possible. You may not know what the source of that inspiration is, though in some ways it doesn't matter. It could be a memory deep inside of a feeling that you've experienced in a relationship, or perhaps it's an experience of witnessing someone else experiencing a very different type of relationship. But whatever it is, we can be grateful that this dream has been ignited somewhere within. Without that, it's doubtful whether we'd ever even have had the thought to make a change.

Like so many struggling, we'd simply say that this is just the way things are as we accept that things are just going to continue like that until the end. Resigned to a miserable relationship, coping as best we can while blaming our partner for their part in our unhappy existence.

When we can't ignore the pain anymore

Have you ever experienced the shift in the way you see a problem - any kind of problem - where the pain of ignoring the problem suddenly becomes greater than the pain of the problem itself. It was the week before your exam when you realised that time had become so squeezed that it really was now or never. Or it could be when someone makes a gentle comment about your weight, and you realise that it wasn't just yourself that noticed that you are carrying too many kilos after the holidays.

In relationships, this tends to be a big event like an explosive argument where we not only lose our temper, but something gets thrown around like an insult or phone or a plate is smashed, and we become aware that next time it could get serious. At that time, we recognise that this issue that has been affecting things for a while has moved into the "too serious to ignore" category.

The building starts to collapse.

Using the building analogy from earlier, this is where the irritations that show up in Stage 3 (the cracks in the wall), develop into a much bigger problem in Stage 4. So rather than have a couple of cracks in the wall that have been papered over, we might be missing an entire wall!

"Well, a bit of extra natural light might be ok", we might consider in one final attempt at denial. "And the fresh air will do us good."

But when we consider its winter, and that's the room where our kids have breakfast, we soon enough must accept the reality that this room really isn't viable any more in its current state. This is the time when some people will move out if they have the means to do so, giving up on the house. In terms of the relationship, the parallel is simple. We consider the relationship not viable anymore, we don't like the look of it, so we move on.

Others will re-commit and say that they really believe in the building but that it needs a different approach to be able to rebuild it on proper foundations. Only then can we rest happy knowing that we have something strong that will stand the test of time and support ourselves and the important people around us.

The most familiar challenges

So, what are the most common issues that show up in relationships, where we become aware that there is an underlying problem and that we're stuck in a cycle of going around in circles?

Your Relationship Feels UNSAFE

We all have an inner "Defender" that is ready to step in if at any point we feel under threat. Have you ever experienced yourself (or even seeing someone we love like a child) in immediate danger? What are the feelings that come up at that time?

Getting ourselves safe from a wild animal

For most of us, the threats that we experience from wild animals are less than they would have been for our ancestors. In our cities the threat might be a stray dog, though for how long would the dog be on the loose before being picked up by the authorities anyway? In the countryside, it's probably livestock that could be the most dangerous, though issues are sufficiently rare that they make the news when they do happen.

The dangers lurking in modern life.

Even though we don't have the same risk profile in terms of animals roaming, what are the modern factors that could trigger us into a feeling that we are in danger? At work we feel that someone is encroaching into our space, causing a negative impact on our work or career prospects. Or in our relationship if our feelings are not acknowledged we feel invalidated and that we effectively don't exist for our partner. We have a sense of losing ourselves and that we are unable to express an opinion or to do something that is important to us. Maybe our authority is challenged by a rebellious teenager, and we feel that we are losing our ability to make decisions in our life. Or maybe because our partner has punished us in the past when they didn't get their way, we now feel that we can't open up and be vulnerable in the way we'd like to be.

Whatever the triggers it's important to realise that issues persist in our lives that have the ability of triggering us into the kind of "get safe now" reaction we may have needed in the past.

High vigilance in response to physical danger

Even though we don't have the threats of the past, we still have a biological makeup very similar to that of our ancestors. If we do find ourselves in danger, we have several stress hormones (primarily adrenaline and cortisol) that kick in and put us on high alert meaning that we are ready to run, climb a tree or fight for our lives. Let's call this a state of high vigilance.

While these responses are useful in certain situations and have contributed to the success and survival of our species, they also come with some drawbacks when we think of the situations that we need to navigate in our modern lives. For instance, if in a disagreement with my partner I get triggered into this state of high vigilance, is it possible that I may not be fully present to my partner and what their needs are at this moment? Could I even do some damage through a reaction made without due care and consideration?

Let's look at these reactions in more detail, so that you can identify which ones tend to be present for you. Each one of these has a high and low reading, which we look at in more detail through our work, especially how the dynamic between our reactions is affecting our relationship and the multiple combinations that can be at play

An *elevated* Fight response means that when we find ourselves in danger we look to confront and defeat that danger head on. Perhaps we hold back and look for the right vulnerability before attacking or we just jump straight in. We might recognise this in situations when we look back at a conflict that we've initiated or joined that when we reflect on it wasn't necessary at all. Maybe there had been a misunderstanding, or we see that with some additional clarification or discussion we could have avoided things kicking off or breaking down.

There could also be a *suppressed* Fight response which may not be so visible as in the first case but can be equally problematic in the longer term. This is where there is a need to "Fight" such as having a proper boundary, or sticking to a key point but that we find ourselves rolling over to avoid the conflict. The hallmark of this is when we create a much bigger issue than the one that would have been caused had we confronted the issue correctly when it arose.

Which one of these sounds more familiar, or perhaps you have a good balance in this area?

An *elevated* Flight response means that we tend to "act first, think later". Have you ever exited a situation (a relationship, or a job) and then come to reflect that it would have been worth sticking around a little longer and working on things? Maybe we've ended up losing something that we really valued and regret that in a rush of blood we've walked away.

A *suppressed* Flight response means that we might be too slow to act or to leave the scene. Have you ever stayed in a job or a relationship too long, way beyond when you really knew that it wasn't working and that a change was necessary. If we have this tendency, it could be that we've stayed way too long before pulling the trigger on an important decision. Can you think of any areas of your life where you might have lost years through preserving something beyond its useful or functional life?

Freeze - there in body, but emotionally disconnected!

With an *elevated* Freeze response, we are triggered emotionally to pull away. We deal with the challenge or threat by "playing dead". In our case, this may not be lying motionless on the floor like we may see in other animals, but it's our modern equivalent of this process. We disengage emotionally to protect ourselves as if we are there in body but not in mind or spirit.

"I'm going to wear my coat of armour," we thought. "That way nobody can hurt us."

While the armour does give us a level of safety, it also has an impact on our ability to really enjoy the fullness of life. Let's say it's a hot day and we hit the beach. Is that coat of armour going to limit our enjoyment of the experience?

A *suppressed* Freeze response means that our degree of emotionality is affected but in the opposite direction. This is where we may become emotionally volatile, for example taking things very personally only to realise later that it really wasn't about us at all. We might lose perspective or even the ability to think because our emotions are so aroused that we can do no other than retreat to our bed or sofa to process our emotions.

Fawn - if I can just help others enough, then everything will be ok!

An *elevated* Fawn response is that we become overly or inappropriately giving to others. We deal with the stress by putting ourselves last, and simply looking for ways to be liked by others. We imagine that if only we can give enough then finally everyone will like us, and our problems will go away. This might feel good for a while, but then often we reach a point where it's unsustainable. We are not meeting our own needs and we have a negative physical or emotional symptom as a result. Or maybe that the people we imagined would also put us first show that they are not willing to support us when we need it, thus leading to resentment or a form of breakdown.

A *suppressed* Fawn response is when we go the other way and deal with the stressful situation by flipping into an overly selfish mode where we disregard other people's feelings and needs. We decide to focus most of our energy on "number one", and this may yield results in the short term as we get ourselves to safety and away from danger. For instance, when the flight crew performs their briefing, who's oxygen mask are we reminded to fit first before trying to help the people around us? While this may make perfect sense again in the immediate context, what impacts could this have if it becomes our default pattern? For instance, how might it affect our partner or other people around us if we always tend to react to difficulties or stress by putting ourselves first?

Boundaries break down.

When we hear from clients about the challenges they are experiencing, in virtually all cases there are aspects of where correct boundaries have broken down. There are some breaches of boundaries that are very visible, especially where threats or intimidation are taking place. Often though there are more subtle ways that boundaries are broken such as through emotional manipulation which can be equally as impactful emotionally, if not physically. When this happens, there are always consequences on the relationship, and often on the state of mind of the people affected.

Focussing in the right areas

Hard work and effort in general are highly valued qualities. But if the effort is going into the wrong areas, it can be frustrating and damaging. We might be trying hard, but if that trying is for instance in looking to control something or somebody that we are not able to control there are likely to be negative impacts. Not only do we create resentment, but we also drain ourselves of energy that could be correctly spent on things that really do sit naturally within our remit!

When we step into other people's business

One of the most common areas of conflict can be when we try to control things that only other people can ultimately decide on. In these cases, even when it's coming from a place of wanting the best for our partner it can quickly lead to resentment. Maybe we know that our partner has been trying to lose weight and we see them tucking into food that we know is not in line with their diet. How easy is it for a simple comment to lead to a sense that we are controlling our partner, and not allowing them to eat what they choose.

"Yes, I know I'm on a diet, but today I just fancy the pizza," they might say. Could it be that a level of disapproval or judgement is expressed that makes them feel uncomfortable and judged and which leads to bad feeling?

When we let other people step into our business

On the flipside, do we ever go along with the attempts of others to prevent us from exercising our choices, and how does that affect the relationship? Is it possible to have a positive and healthy relationship when the lines become blurred in this way, or will we inevitably have a level of resentment leading to a breakdown of trust and connection?

We are going to be looking later at a model to enable us to get really clear on where healthy boundaries lie and how to ensure that we can easily identify any breaches of those boundaries that may be taking place.

Communication is difficult.

One of the most reported challenges when people reach out for support is that a couple is unable to communicate effectively.

"That's interesting because I can understand every word you are saying," we might respond.

As well as being a light-hearted way to shift the mood, there is a more serious point here too. We may certainly have the feeling that we are just unable to communicate but what are the causes of those relationship challenges?

So, what are the distinct types of communication difficulties that show up when we are struggling in our relationship?

A pattern of pervading negativity

One of the ways that communication can break down is through the influence of persistent and unnecessary negativity. Nothing is good enough and every effort we make seems to be shot down. We might get to the point where even as we weigh up the options in our mind of how to respond to something, or to raise a concern there appears no viable way of negotiating it without triggering a negative response.

"If I do A I'm stuffed, and if I do B I'm also in trouble," we might think.

This is a function of the emotional state that we or our partner - or more likely both - are in, and it's a key area that we address through our work with couples and individuals to improve their relationships. The challenge is that it can be a habit or pattern that stretches back a long way, and we may even lose the perspective that an alternative way of communicating is even possible.

"That's just the way I speak, that's who I am," we might say.

The issue is that nothing good is going to happen in the relationship (or even in our lives) if we value being happy, until we shift this pattern.

Let's take an example to illustrate. If your partner (or anyone for that matter) makes a negative point such as:

"I can't believe these immigrants, coming here and not even being willing to do a day's work," for instance. At this point if you decide to engage with the conversation, you've got two options. Firstly, you could state the counter point:

"Well, I've met loads of immigrants, and I know that they are not only really nice people but also very hard working so no I don't agree with that at all."

How might the other person react at that point? Do they welcome debate with an openness to hearing a different point of view? Or do they get defensive or dismissive leading to an argument or the conversation breaking down?

The second option we have is to appease or to pacify the person by going along with the negative comment and buying into it.

"Yes, I know what you mean, I read about this case where these people came here then just started claiming benefits," we might chime in.

So, what happens? Does that resolve or alleviate the negativity, or does it just embed it even further? This is the typical challenge when we think to ourselves that we just can't win, and it can lead to communication breaking down or feeling like a waste of time. Soon we might even give up on the idea that talking about things at all is going to lead to improvements, so we withdraw completely.

And this doesn't mean that we need to be deluded or starry-eyed either. It's not that we can't have our eyes open to recognise when people have agendas or objectives that don't fit with our own. We can maintain a healthy perspective and recognise that to stay safe it may be useful to put in place a level of self-protection. The question is do we want to let ourselves be taken over by that pervading fear or negativity that some people - and much of the media for that matter - have decided to set up as our primary operating system?

Positioning for control

Another way that communication can become difficult is when we are both trying to lead or control a situation at the same time, battling for the control of something. The same challenge can come up at work - especially with colleagues who may be in different teams or at the same level in the organisational hierarchy. It's the same reason why it's not recommended that if you decide to have two puppies from the same litter - they are always likely to be vying for leadership and dominance, just like we could jostle for control with a colleague from another team.

If you take the analogy of non-choreographed couples dancing such as salsa or bachata dancing. So long as you have a partner ready to lead the dance, and another willing to be led the dancing works. And it's not gender-dependent either - a couple of any gender combination can dance successfully so long as they adopt these roles which we will look at in more detail later.

If BOTH decide to lead at the same time though, we can confidently predict what is going to happen and how the dance is going to break down! One thinks we're going this way, and the other has another plan completely! It's simply not possible for both to get their way in that moment and to continue dancing successfully together!

A difference in pace

We have distinctive styles of processing information, and some of us may like to move quickly while others need more time to reflect and process.

"Come on, what are we waiting for - we need to make a decision NOW", one partner might say.

"Hang on, I haven't finished gathering data yet on which I'm going to be able to make a decision," the other might respond.

There is an amusing scene in the film Zootopia when Officer Judy is dealing with Flash the sloth in the council offices which demonstrates what can happen! Look it up online if you haven't seen it.

There is no ultimate right and wrong in this dilemma and it's likely to be context dependent. Sometimes a quick decision might bring big benefits or even allow us to solve a problem that we will otherwise not be able to do. For instance, in the army if we are reacting in the face of an enemy assault, it could be necessary to move quickly perhaps to stop ourselves from being surrounded.

At other times there may be real benefits in stopping and evaluating before making a big decision. It might be worth looking through the exam results of different schools that we are proposing to send our child, rather than looking to make a quick decision based on something like location.

The challenges are in the grey areas where for example in buying a house there are important considerations to evaluate like doing market research about an area that you are considering moving to. On the flipside, once a house comes on the market, there may be other people interested, meaning that there is a 'first mover advantage' to be gained too. So, like in so many areas we dive into, 'it depends'.

Following the rules versus the 'Rebel'?

Some of us tend towards wanting to follow the rules and to "do things by the book". We consider it a mark of respect, or we could also gain some certainty or confidence from knowing that if we encounter a problem, we can always fall back on the rulebook to justify what we've done.

Others struggle with rulebooks and might even feel a level of repulsion like an allergic reaction to having to follow the rules.

"Thanks for letting me know that there are rules," we might say. "But I think you may have mistaken me for someone who CARES about the rules... Now leave me alone to do it my way!"

Again, both approaches can lead to challenges and it's really context dependent. If you try to follow a complex procedure such as putting together a complicated flat pack of furniture, then ignoring the instructions could be a fast-track to an extended period of confusion, frustration, and re-work!

On the other hand, there are situations in which rigidly adhering to the process could be unnecessary and increase the time and cost of achieving our goal.

When we lack a common language

It might sound like the most obvious point, but if we don't have a common language that we can both fluently express ourselves in, this could have an impact on our ability to communicate.

We previously had clients where while they did have a shared language, one of them spoke the language to a more basic or functional level which meant that there were nuances or aspects that were difficult to convey or 'lost in translation'.

We've entered the "power struggle".

When we first meet a partner, we can tend to overlook or minimise the challenges that we are presented with. Our partner makes a sarcastic comment, and we pass it off lightly that she's just having one of those difficult days. Lovely them, they didn't really mean it. Or maybe they leave a mess in the kitchen, and we happily spend time clearing it up, feeling connected to them and thinking how we're making their life easier by supporting them.

But then we get to a point where we can no longer ignore those challenges and we are forced to confront them. This phase has been described as the "power struggle"[15]. During this time, we must confront and overcome these differences, getting issues out in the open that had previously been ignored or brushed over. It's like they can't be ignored any more, and often the raising of one challenge will lead to the uncovering of another.

A friend shared a situation at university where they had been taking turns cooking evening meals for others in the house. Things had been going quite well with everyone fitting in and eating the food presented by

---

[15] Harville Hendrix, Finding Lasting Love.

housemates. Then one day, the first person couldn't hold back anymore.

"I've got to say, I really don't like this meal very much." the brave person said.

This opened the proverbial can of worms, and many of the housemates then raised their own issues - bottled up until then - of issues with other people's meals. Before long the whole meal-sharing experiment was over, and they reverted to cooking their own meals!

A similar phenomenon can happen at this stage in relationships too where issues are finally brought to the surface leading to an avalanche of counterclaims and related problems.

There is no love in the relationship.

"Of course, we love each other," we might think. "We've got these amazing kids and we're here sharing this space, so that must be a kind of love, right?" But what needs to be happening, or what do we need to experience to be able to say that a relationship is really a loving one, rather than a functional one or even an abusive one?

Do we support each other to meet our needs?

When people reach out for support with their relationship, there is always an element of unmet needs that are affecting one or normally both partners. If all our needs were being consistently met at a high level, we'd be experiencing the kind of life that we want, and we would be happy and satisfied. This is one of the perspectives that we use to help clients make sense of where things may be not working as well as we want them to.

Some of us may be good at supporting our partner to meet their needs - always thinking of them and finding ways to support them. We believe that by putting our partner (or others) first that they will naturally and automatically do the same for us.

Others are better at ensuring our own needs are met, and that we are individually in a good place. However, we may not be as quick to identify, or recognise or to act to support our partner to meet their needs. We may find ways to support, but it doesn't come as easily or naturally as our ability to focus on ourselves.

Whatever balance we strike here, what would it be saying if our partner showed little or no interest at all in supporting us to meet our needs? Maybe they even see us struggling or unhappy, but they carry on regardless with what they are doing. Like we are not there, they are oblivious to our challenges. What does this say about the level of care or love they feel towards us, at least at that point?

Would a loving relationship make sense if we don't take interest or support each other to meet each other's needs?

Do we try to accept each other the way we are?

"Well sure I do want my partner to change in a few ways," we might think. "But it's only for their own good - they'll be happier that way, more relaxed and they'll get on better with people."

Perhaps we'd like them to be more patient, to not raise their voice when they get upset or simply to be more considerate when they are getting ready for work so that they don't wake us up unnecessarily. We might even have asked them about these concerns, and they may have tried to address them, only to revert to the original behaviour which we find difficult to accept.

What is the impact on the relationship of having a sense of being unacceptable to our partner the way we are? Does that give us a feeling of warmth and love to know that we have qualities or behaviours that our partner finds challenging or defective in some way. Maybe they are even embarrassed by those things and find it difficult to be seen alongside us.

Do we keep score?

Most of our relationships or interactions in life have a sense of measurement attached to them, where a transaction is occurring. If we are employed for instance, we have an agreement that we perform certain duties, and in exchange we are paid an agreed sum as well as having other benefits such as paid leave. Or if we go into a shop, we expect to exchange a set sum of money for goods or services.

We give something in return for receiving something - sometimes this will be written in a contract or agreement, or it may otherwise be just implicitly understood that this is the deal.

How about in our loving or intimate relationships? Do we still have a sense of doing something with an expectation of a return or are we able to give freely, knowing that our partner also has the flexibility to support where we have that need.

"Hang on, today was your turn to clean and I can still see dirt in the bathroom!", one person might say.

"Well, I did do my part of the cleaning but THAT mess you are referring to was still there from last week when you were meant to do the cleaning but only did half a job!", the other retorts.

And it might seem a stretch to completely let go of this part of us that is so ingrained that is always counting and evaluating. However, do we at least aspire to a loving relationship where it's not primarily governed by a written or unwritten deal of what we are willing to do, in exchange for things being done in return? What would be the alternative?

Do we ask or expect our partner to do things they don't want to do?

Elevated expectations are sometimes referenced as a positive, but what if the elevated expectations are relating to someone else rather than ourselves?

"I just want my partner to be the best version of themself," we might rationalise.

Also, this can be coming from an apparent motivation of wanting to help or support the other person. And again, if the drive for change has come from the other person, then it could be beneficial to support them in finding resources or to encourage them in the direction of the change.

If this drive leads to a pressure, on the other hand, for your partner to have to do things that they don't want to do then what kind of feelings are likely to be coming up for them? Is a sense of expectation or having to do something or achieve something to keep the other person happy a great basis for the connection that we are looking for?

You have dependency issues.

Throughout our childhood and development - and especially at the beginning - we are highly dependent on the people and the world around us to keep us safe. A baby clearly has no means of looking after themself, so part of the natural order is that until we can function independently, other people ensure our safe and effective development.

As we grow and mature, we take more responsibility, starting by managing a small amount of pocket money and some autonomy to go where we choose with our friends. Then we find ways to express our independence more fully as we determine our path in life, the work we choose, our values and the people we decide to spend time around.

But what happens when the process doesn't reach completion, and we struggle to function independently? Could this lead to relationship challenges as we move into adulthood?

We struggle to function independently.

As we develop our relationship, it's perfectly normal to depend on our partner in many ways. Whether it's through practical support day to day, or even supporting us emotionally when we are struggling. Our lives are intertwined, and many of the moving parts will interface between us. Let's say that one partner has children from a previous relationship, then the interaction with a new partner is likely to be not only unavoidable but also desirable. We want connection with our partner, and our children are in a sense an extension of ourselves.

There is an important line however in recognising that we are at least <u>capable</u> of functioning independently. If we convey a sense that our lives would simply cease to work if our partner wasn't there to prop us up, this could lead to an uncomfortable dependency. Is our partner responsible for us in this way, in the same way that a parent might once have been?

We don't take responsibility for our own feelings.

A young child in distress can expect to be comforted lovingly by a parent or authority figure, rather than to be abandoned and neglected. A simple hug could be all that's needed to make the pain of the fall go away. We're not physically hurt but we do feel emotionally upset and when we are soothed in that way, we quickly put a brave face back on in most cases.

If we see our partner feeling upset or vulnerable, then we might be able to provide comfort and support. At that time, it may feel like we're in a parent-type role, and in another situation, roles may be reversed as we ourselves are comforted in a moment of distress. For many, the sense of emotional support is an important aspect that we are looking for in a relationship. Our partner knows us well and can identify and support us in situations that we might otherwise struggle with.

While it may be a wonderful thing when our partner is able to support us emotionally, a step beyond is when we make our partner responsible for our feelings. Can our partner always be available to identify and soothe us when we are in need, to be attentive and even to predict when we may be in distress? If we were to place that expectation on our partner, what kind of relationship could that begin to resemble?

We look to control someone else to feel in control.

Our feelings of vulnerability and need can be addressed in several ways. One would be to focus on things that are within our remit and to mitigate any perceived risks to the best of our ability. Another would be to focus on our partner and look for that reassurance by looking to control them.

How does it feel when our autonomy to operate is limited by the expectation of our partner that we support them to feel in control by acting in a certain way? And does it even work? When we look to exert control over external factors like our partner, do we still have this nagging feeling that we are on shaky ground and that the person might follow their own path in any case?

A client had asked for a book recommendation to give him some additional understanding of an area of the relationship that he was working on. After receiving the book through the post he'd dived in at which point his wife took an interest and asked him what he was reading.

He showed it to her, and suddenly her mood changed:

"I can't believe that you would do this to me, I'm really upset now", she said, breaking down emotionally into sobs and tears.

Taken aback he put the book back into the packaging and reassured her that he wouldn't be reading it anymore if she felt upset by it. This was what she was looking for, as her emotions quickly returned to normal, and she calmed herself down regaining her composure.

Our self-esteem depends on someone else.

If we have grown up without the positive affirmation that we were looking for, a disempowering script can be written that follows us throughout our life. This can easily then show up in our relationships where we are looking to find that kind of reassurance through our partner. That search for affirmation or acceptance from others - such as our partner - can lead to reactions and behaviours that are uncomfortable or dysfunctional.

We haven't learnt to stand alone.

While a baby only identifies themself as a separate individual from their mother at the age of six months, the process of truly breaking away from the parents is a journey through childhood and adolescence. In the animal kingdom there is often a time when a youngster splits away from the parents to find their own way in the world. In human development it's usually a less visible break between child and parent and even though we may be living separately, we maintain contact and possibly elements of support for many years. Depending on culture, even the physical split of living in separate places is long delayed for financial or other reasons.

What happens when this splitting process - sometimes called individuation - doesn't complete and we become entangled with our parents or caregivers and fail to find our own authentic voice? We struggle to question ideas that have been handed down to us, and just accept them as the way things are.

In a relationship both partners bring a legacy of experience, ideas and other resources to the table and the relationship can be seen as a third entity that is created. It is not the same as either of the individual legacies but something new. It's like a cake isn't the same as any of the individual ingredients - the flour, sugar, oil and so on - but a separate thing that is born through the mixing and baking process.

So, if we haven't yet fully formed ourselves from the journey of childhood and adolescence it can be like the ingredients that we bring are not fully formed but rather unstable. It's like during the baking process that the cocoa powder that we brought to the recipe is unstable and shifts to something unexpected mid-way through its time in the oven.

"I thought we'd talked about this and agreed that it would make sense for us to live in this city for now, at least until I finish this project and we can rethink", we might say.

"Yeah, but I've talked about it with my mum & dad, and they want me closer to them," our partner responds.

What happens when we are not able to operate independently and make our own decisions, and could it feel like there is an additional person or persons in the relationship pulling the strings? Like we can't fully commit to any decision without asking permission from someone else first.

The relationship seems to take away your freedom.
We may have witnessed situations in which someone close to us seemed to lose freedom through their participation in a relationship. Rather than a creative journey of support and building something greater than the whole, in these relationships it feels like something is being restricted or suffocated. The person loses autonomy and thus self-confidence or they lose their independence.

If this was the case, what kind of beliefs or ideas might we have internalised about relationships and the things we need to be wary of in avoiding the same fate ourselves.

Anna's parents had a difficult relationship, and she had witnessed her father's behaviour at close quarters including the effect on her mother. He had gone through a series of affairs and extra-marital relationships which had sometimes become known and led to serious conflicts between Anna's parents. Anna had witnessed her mother broken by the breaches of trust, always willing to give him another chance despite her sadness and sense of betrayal.

"Mum, why don't you leave?" Anna would remonstrate seeing her so low. "You deserve better, and you shouldn't let him do that to you. Together we can make a new life, and I'm with you."

Despite her best efforts of support and encouragement, Anna's mother never in fact took the step of moving on but chose to persist unhappily with the relationship. This left Anna frustrated at seeing her mother so unhappy but trapped and becoming a shell of the person she once was.

"This will NEVER happen to me", Anna now tells herself with complete certainty and conviction.

How could this experience and narrative play into her own relationships, or our own relationship? Could it be that she finds a situation to enable her to right the wrongs of the past? Could we replay the story that we've witnessed while changing the ending on behalf of the person we saw trapped? How might this affect the narrative of our own life and is our partner even behaving in the same way as we saw earlier in the other person's story?

The impact on our relationship

As described, these habits will often be based on challenges that we've experienced growing up that haven't been fully recognised and healed. For all of us, there would have been moments when we needed support, but that support wasn't available for any number of reasons. And how we experience these challenges is a very personal matter, due to our level of maturity and sensitivity. Two people could go through a similar looking experience but process and recall it in a completely unique way.

It may be that by simply recognising these challenges and considering the impact that they have had on our relationships that we are ready to move on. If we are struggling in this area, it may be something that we want to explore in therapy.

Things have got mundane and flat.

Up until surprisingly recently, the idea that our marriages and relationships had a purpose of giving us love, connection and excitement would not have figured in our expectations. For centuries marriage has been framed more around being a model of family organisation and economics whereby we work together to raise our children. It would also be a convenient way to see who would inherit the family resources, and the lines of work that we would often follow our parents into. It was only in the twentieth century that the idea was really established in our culture that our marriages should give us deep connection, romance, and love. Up until then we had our passion outside of our marriage, or not at all.[16]

Despite this, we now generally have higher expectations of our relationships than simply being a way to organise ourselves economically and to effectively raise children. So, what happens when these expectations are not met?

We never do anything new or exciting.

In the same way that most jobs will have their boring or repetitive elements, it's likely that our domestic responsibilities would include things that don't fill us with joy. The bills need to be paid and the house needs to be cleaned and maintained. You may be one of those rare people who really enjoy these activities though for many of us it can feel like a long way from the excitement of the start of the relationship!

But what happens in the relationship when all we can see is domestic life stretching out to the horizon and there are no fun or exciting things to break the monotony? Do you ever dream of going somewhere

---

[16] Mating in Captivity by Esther Perel

new, or changing your environment or moving to live in a different place altogether?

We've lost the spark and feel more like flatmates.

Two flatmates could get along fine, and the relationship could function well in terms of sharing the building and living out our lives. We even do activities together like watching TV or having a meal together, but there is an understanding that lives are still substantially separate. When it's convenient we can do things together, but beyond that we'll operate as individual entities.

"You pay this bill, and I'll pay the other and we each pay half towards the rent," we might agree.

So far, so good, and some flatmates can live happily together for a long time. But what if we are looking for more from our relationship than simply to co-exist under the same roof? We long for a deeper connection and spark than the arrangement of flatmates can allow.

I can't get excited about our future.

How differently we feel when we have a sense of clarity about where we are going. It's like the difference between driving knowing our destination and why we are setting out on that journey, versus just getting in the car and driving around for a while aimlessly! Perhaps you can just relax driving or enjoy the views, though for many this would soon feel like a waste of time.

Maybe we have this clarity and excitement in some areas of life such as at work, but less so in our family or relationship. So, what happens in our relationship when we don't have that sense of where we are going, and we feel that we are just aimlessly drifting? Or the things that we are spending our time doing have lost or simply lack real connection or meaning for us?

If we either don't understand or can't buy into this direction of travel, how might this affect us? Do the mundane but necessary tasks become frustrating when we don't have a sense of our longer-term goal or frustration? Could we end up lacking passion or motivation or even become frustrated? If we do, how might that then play out in our relationship?

We don't have sexual chemistry.

Is mundanity and boredom conducive to sexual spark or does it leave us flat and uninterested? When are we overly domesticated does our sexual drive sustain itself or could it decline over time?

In sharing domestic space, it's common that we see each other in ways that we would not necessarily present ourselves to the outside world. As our partner drags themselves to the kitchen for the first coffee of the day, it's possible that they are not looking as alluring as they did the previous night as they arrived at the bar!

This can have a cumulative effect over time, as any mystery is stripped away and the reality of our partner - including all their unpleasant habits - is laid bare!

In addition, as we spend more time together, we tend to lose some of the magnetism that made it feel exciting when we were first intimate with our partner. Like two magnets that are left in proximity, they eventually lose the magnetism and are eventually just two pieces of iron next to one another. No spark and no attraction.

This isn't to say that sex doesn't work at all. It could be that things still function, but what we've lost is the magic and spark and we feel that as a lack of connection.

The impact on our relationship

If things have become mundane and flat, what do we do to relieve ourselves of that boredom? Could things be set in place to overcome this challenge that are harmful to the relationship, or to have unintended side effects?

Your needs are not being met.

Another angle that we look at closely through our work with couples and individuals to improve their relationship is to look at what unmet needs we might be having. If we are struggling, then we can say with confidence that one or more needs are not being met at a level that we would be satisfied with. Otherwise, we'd be thriving, content and happy. So, what are those key needs that we can evaluate to better understand the gaps that we are experiencing?

The difference between having an unmet need and meeting that need effectively can be startling. Have you ever found yourself on holiday after not being away for *ages*, standing with a slightly giddy smile on your face thinking, "Wow, I didn't realise how much I needed this?" How does this change the quality of your life to meet a need at a high level versus when we have unmet needs, especially over a significant period?

One of the most famous models in this area is known as Maslow's hierarchy of needs created in the 1940s, and it has been developed and expanded over the years by several other writers in the field of psychology[17]. It is often presented as a pyramid with the more basic needs at the bottom, and this framework is developed below with a relationship focus.

Also, to note that while we ALL have the following needs to some extent, we may experience this to different intensities and in some cases may say that a need is of lower or minor importance for ourselves.

17

https://en.wikipedia.org/wiki/Maslow%27s_hierarchy_of_need s

Unmet need 1 - We feel uncertain, insecure, or unsafe.

We all have fundamental needs to function, and this need relates to the bottom two tiers of Maslow's pyramid. This includes our need for food and shelter and sufficient income to function at a satisfactory level. It's about our ability to sustain ourselves and to stay safe.

If this need is not being met in our relationship, we may be reflecting on whether the relationship is even going to survive and how our lives might look if it were to fail. For instance, where am I going to live, and would I have the resources to sustain my life and the life of the people around me?

A client shared how one of the go-to reactions from his partner during the back and forth of their regular arguments was that,

"If we are unable to agree then you might as well leave."

As the house that they lived together in was owned by one partner (the other had rented their house out after he had moved in), this would lead him effectively to homelessness. In fact, after these arguments he would sometimes leave the house and walk the streets reflecting on how unstable the relationship was and coming up with contingency plans of where he could stay if his partner didn't let him back into the house.

100

Unmet need 2 - We feel boredom or a lack of excitement.

From the first need we can see that there is a level of stability and safety that we must have in place if we are going to function effectively. Once this is met though, there can be a level of stability that flips into another quite different problem - that of boredom. While some people can tolerate this better and for longer, we all need a degree of variety and difference in our daily schedule if we are going to avoid things feeling stale.

John and Sarah reflected that due to their busy lives and different schedules - especially since their son was born the previous year - that they never did the things that they used to enjoy together, and which brought the fun and spark into the relationship. Too much sameness in their schedule had led them to a point where it was difficult to get excited about things or to look forward to plans together. Everything just felt flat and domesticated.

Unmet need 3 - We feel unloved or lonely.

It's no coincidence that one of the most well-known forms of punishment or torture is through the removal of human contact from a person[18]. We humans are social animals, and a great deal of distress can be created in a short space of time when we don't have this social

---

[18] https://howardleague.org/legal-work/solitary-confinement/

contact. It's likely that this response comes from our evolution whereby being excluded from our family or society and cast into the wilderness would have left us little chance of survival.

For many of us, the need to feel loved and connected to others is a need that we want to meet at least to some extent in our relationship with our partner. It's also worth noting that we can meet this need through a variety of social contact with friends and family, as well as through our pets. It may be that a couple both have this need to a high level but prefer to meet it in different ways, which are culturally informed. For instance, in some cultures the mother-daughter(s) bond is strongly maintained through life whereas in other cultures it would be expected that this would be reduced post-marriage.

In a previous unhappy relationship, I became much clearer that my need for feeling loved was not being met through a fortunate coincidence. While I was certainly aware that I was missing something, I'd become used to having minimal love and affection over many years, so I'd got settled in an unhappy rut.

"That's just the way she is," I thought, while putting my own unhappiness to one side.

I was working away from home, and I was staying short term with a friend who happened to live with her dog, Joey. I connected with the dog and after a few days of living there, you can guess what kind of reaction I would get from Joey when I came back home after a long day in the office! This really affected me on a deep level and like the holiday example earlier, I felt the contrast in reaction between Joey and my ex-partner. How happy he would be to see me compared to the reaction I would get from my ex-partner for years when I came home - sometimes after working away for a period supporting the people around me.

In those cases, I'd be lucky if she looked up from her magazine or TV programme when I came home - whereas Joey was almost overcome by excitement at being able to greet me to the house! This was such a gift as it enabled me to clarify not only the idea that I was unhappy but to really feel the difference when this need was met - at least to a much higher level than it had been met previously! It was like the thawing of the permafrost that had set in, and enabled emotions that had been frozen away for years to come flowing back, like re-awakening a part of myself that had been long forgotten.

Unmet need 4 - We feel invisible or insignificant.

There are several ways that we feel recognised by other people, whether it's in winning an award or simply in positive feedback of a job well done. We can also reflect on our achievements and give ourselves the proverbial pat on the back, even without other people's input. However, as social creatures there are few of us who are genuinely unaffected by the praise and recognition of others!

There are several areas of our lives where we may be made to feel significant and recognised. It may be that our boss or colleagues at work give us positive feedback and outwardly appreciate our work. We may feel the glow of appreciation from our neighbours of that new car which could be seen by them as a symbol of achievement. Or it could be that our partner or family expresses gratitude for our hard work to support them.

"What do you mean it would be nice to say thank you from time to time," a client shared that his wife would remonstrate. "It's not that you're doing anything out of the ordinary AT ALL. You're just fulfilling the responsibilities that ANY father must do."

This man was a hardworking, level-headed, and loyal partner. He wasn't claiming to be perfect, but the basic facts of the situation were worth keeping in mind. While both partners worked, his skills and experience meant that in their case he earned something like ninety percent of the household income. He carried this with good grace and didn't mind at all that he would not only support the lifestyle requirements of the family - regular holidays and international travel for instance - but would be ready to support the household however he could day to day as well.

This client worked away for much of the time, meaning that at those times childcare would sit more with his wife, and she did a tremendous job supported by other family members and a flexible working environment. However, when he was home, he would cook and clean, do the dishes and laundry and lead with the childcare to let his wife rest as much as possible.

At the same time, he wasn't claiming to be a saint, and recognised that he could sometimes be inconsiderate or get it wrong in different ways. He was open to working on those aspects and coming to a clearer understanding.

However, there was no accusation from his wife or anyone else of any gross misbehaviour on his part. He hadn't cheated on her, he didn't lose his temper in a rage, he didn't gamble away the family's money and he didn't come home in a drunken stupor. In fact, he didn't drink at all and rarely went out with friends as he didn't have many friends in that part of the country. Indeed, they had relocated there away from where they previously lived to be closer to her family and friends.

"I just don't know what more I can do, it's never enough!", he said. "It's like when I bring the groceries back, let's say there's 100 things on her list and I get 99 of them. All I hear about is the one thing that I couldn't find."

What would be the impact on this person of that constant nagging feeling that whatever they do, it's not enough. Could they even start doubting themselves and believing that perspective that they were uncaring or defective in some way? Even as he keeps going the extra mile to please his wife, is there any guarantee whatsoever that she will eventually recognise anything that he does to support?

Unmet need 5 - We feel stagnant and stuck.

Every day we are alive we can say that we're a day closer to the day we die. And while death is a taboo subject in our culture, don't we all sense that we're here for some kind of purpose? Most of the time we distract ourselves with TV and so on, but even then, are there not those quiet moments where we doubt whether we are doing the things that bring us the meaning and happiness that we crave? Are the challenges we face moving us in the direction of something meaningful or are we stuck in a kind of Groundhog Day, repeating the same pattern repeatedly?

One of the areas we look at with clients is how we get stuck in a cycle of negativity and what we need to do to remove ourselves from that cycle!

"I can't believe that we're still having this argument, going around in circles," many will say when they come along to meet us. "I just can't go on with this!"

One way to look at this feeling is to consider our need for growth. As with the other needs, each of us may experience in diverse ways and to greater or lesser extent. But don't we all on some level only feel good about our relationships and our lives in general when we have a sense that we are moving towards something meaningful.

When we were growing up, we observed the world around us, and consciously or unconsciously formed dreams of the life we wanted to create. It was something we saw in a film, or it was through directly observing something in the world around us like the way our parents or caregivers were interacting. The observation could have been formed through a sense of "Yes, I really WANT that", or at other times it could have been more like, "No, I definitely DON'T want that!"

Could it be that our reason for being in the world is to have these kinds of dreams and then to act in the direction of those dreams?[19] When we perceive a gap or shortfall between what we are experiencing at this moment and that dream that we are holding, we experience emotions. In the best case, this could be a resolve or a commitment to be resolute in pursuing something we have identified as valuable.

On the flipside there could also be frustration or even desperation with a sense that, "this just isn't what I'd

---

[19] Ester Hicks, The Vortex describes this process.

imagined for myself". If we feel that the gap is stubbornly large and that we feel that we are not closing the gap, how could those emotions be affecting us day to day, including in our relationships?

Not enough information or not enough implementation?

One perspective on this challenge is whether in the area that we perceive this gap, is to consider whether we are suffering from a lack of understanding or information or whether we have the information that we need but are not acting on that information correctly or consistently.

If we decide that rather than relying on a mechanic, we are going to maintain our own car, there is a good chance that we might struggle without learning some skills at the outset. Imagine opening the bonnet and thinking to yourself, "No it's ok I can figure this out if I just tinker around." We might learn from talking to a mechanic, watching some videos, or doing a course and it's at least possible we might struggle - and even create a few additional problems - until we learn those skills. This is the sense that we need more understanding or information to succeed.

In other cases, we may have already done the courses, got the qualifications but we just don't seem to be able to put things into place. Like we know what to do, but we are not acting consistently in that direction. What we need in this case is not more information but to understand what is holding us back, and to have accountability and support to implement what we already know. Blockages around health and fitness are often in this category, especially since the strategies are not overly complicated. There are two areas that we need to consider - diet and exercise - and most of us know what we are doing and not doing. The issue is more that we don't WANT to know!

Unmet need 6 - We feel unable to share our gifts.

There are many ways that we can get a positive sense of contribution to the world around us. It could be through our work or career that we feel able to give something worthwhile to our team or customers. Others focus on voluntary work in the community that we feel is making the world a better place in a way that is meaningful to us. We can also support our friends and colleagues in giving support when it is needed. And our sense of giving back can also be strengthened by a sense of contributing to our partner and family.

Many of us experience a sense of satisfaction and meaning in seeing others accepting and benefiting from the gifts that we offer.

On the flipside, the sense of having a gift of value but not being able to give it because it's not welcome or appreciated can be a frustrating experience. Imagine bringing a gift to a dinner party, only for the host to say, "no thank you". What does the person need to believe about the gift to not accept it? If we really believe that the gift is valuable, what are we eventually going to do with that gift if we want to experience the sense of completion through seeing someone enjoying that gift?

The Six Levels of Relationship

We have a six-step model for understanding where we are currently starting from which can give us a useful benchmark of the journey we need to go on. Which of the following resonates the most for you, and what do you take away from the upper levels that would be appealing for you to work towards?

Level 1 - My relationship is a war zone.

The image to consider here is of two combatants engaging in a battle. The two protagonists face off to each other on the battlefield, then on the whistle or horn they advance using all means at their disposal - fair or otherwise - to beat the enemy into submission. The choices of weapons will vary depending on their resources and technological advancement, but the dynamic is the same.

It's a matter of identifying the enemy's weakness then putting our tools to use to weaken and then to force the enemy into conceding defeat. At that point, if not put to the sword the loser may be spared their lives, or they may be tormented or tortured further until the victor decides to allow the loser to live another day. Disfigurement is another option where some constraint is imposed like a physical or emotional mark being left, or another condition such as being confined or imprisoned in some way. There is a punishment for daring to rise, like being paraded in public in a humiliating way so that others can throw tomatoes to complete the humiliation.

In the case of our relationship, the means of battle might be more subtle - while confrontations can become physical much more often it's the verbal, emotional and psychological battle that takes place. These battles can still leave scars. Imagine if we have the sense of being battle-hardened or battle-scarred. Are we likely to want to be vulnerable or emotionally open with a person that we feel has inflicted those injuries?

More often with this dynamic we are like the wounded war lord, whose pride is shaken by adversity in battle, and we are simply re-grouping and biding our time for the counter-offensive. We haven't given up, we've just made a temporary retreat to assess our injuries, to count our dead and possibly to summon other resources from elsewhere so that we have a better result next time. For now, we gather ourselves, reflect on our resentment and ready ourselves for the next showdown.

Is it possible that for as long as we are engaging in war, we could be injured or depleted in some way? Are we able to sustain ourselves and our lives here or do we in some sense become less at least in terms of our ability to engage in the relationship or in our life. We may become a powerful warrior but does that in any way empower or enable us to have an effective relationship - especially with the person with whom we are engaging in battle. Could we reach a point where the idea of any positive or emotional relationship with a person who has injured us in this way simply becomes an impossibility? And the longer and more intense the combat, the higher the possibility of us reaching this point of no return.

Level 2 - My relationship is codependent.

At the second level, our relationship is still damaging even though in certain respects we are emotionally closer than we are at level 1. You can think of relationships where couples have in a sense supported each other, but in effect supported each other in destructive habits. Sometimes this can include an element of addiction, such as in the case of Amy Winehouse and her husband Blake, as recounted in a well-known documentary[20].

While in the case of drug addiction it's clear to observe the negative effects - both physical and emotional - the forms of addiction can be more subtle. For instance, we often see a situation where one partner is addicted to a substance such as alcohol or to a habit such as

---

[20] https://www.youtube.com/watch?v=_2yClwmNuLE

gambling, and the other partner is addicted to taking care of that partner.

Kyle is a heavy drinker, and often must be rescued by Chloe when close to unconsciousness in the street or passed out somewhere after a heavy session. Or she would be there the next day to support him with his hangover, as well as taking care of their young daughter. He knows that he can rely on her - she will always be there to support me through those challenges, and they would build a real connection, he thinks.

He sometimes shares his dreams of how he'd like to travel the world, but so far, it's never come to anything and that would be on hold for now in any case. Just getting himself to the shops in one piece was enough of a challenge at times, he thought. Never mind going any further than that.

Does this dynamic lead Kyle towards recovery and taking responsibility for himself, or does it mean that consciously or unconsciously he is more invested in the status quo? It's like their bond is formed through the process of her saving him from himself. Is it possible that he could somehow want to keep this dynamic going, and therefore find ways to sabotage or give up on any avenues of recovery? If he really recovered, the caretaking mother figure would need to find someone else to take care of?

Chloe would worry about Kyle and often tell him that he needs to get himself together, but she also feels needed and significant when she steps in to rescue Kyle. She loves to feel important, and she knows that Kyle is only able to keep himself together with her input.

"Surely I owe it to our daughter to support him to be able to show up as a father - at least some of the time - in a state where he can be a good role model to her?", she thinks.

Chloe is making the right noises about wanting Kyle to recover too, doing her research, and even finding different sources of help that Kyle could access. She just hasn't found the right answer so far, she thinks. But that's ok, it's just a question of time - just keep trying.

But is there another level where she knows that if Kyle really DID recover, then maybe he wouldn't need to be propped up by her anymore? If their connection and relationship is based on his needing her support, what would happen if he really could be independent? Would he still want to be with her, or he'd finally step up to follow his dream that he's always talked about. She'd wake up one day to find that he's really gone to travel the world, and that he didn't want 'mum' along with him.

Is this a dynamic where either Kyle or Chloe is likely to recover and reach their true potential? Or are they both invested in a dysfunctional dance where they are both stuck, trapped in a toxic relationship limiting their growth and evolution as people?

Level 3 - We function like flatmates.

At this level we have a sense that we are sharing a building and a few bills but little else. We may pass some words as we each make breakfast and go on with our day. There is little if any alignment between our goals other than the fact that we've decided to live together under the same roof for the moment.

We may be "good flatmates", where we are mainly considerate and thoughtful, pulling our weight in keeping things in good order resulting in a level of fondness and goodwill. We do our own washing up and take turns to clean the communal areas of the house, but we are clear that we also have our own space. If this space is threatened or challenged, boundaries are soon put in place including locks on doors and so on.

Where things break down, those boundaries could be taken to the next level, taking more rigorous action like keeping our personal things safe through locks on certain doors or keeping things private to avoid unwanted interference.

In addition, unless we've got together overtly as flatmates there is a chance that some frustration could set in with this arrangement. "Is this really what a relationship should be like," we ask ourselves as we look at the other person sensing that they feel like a virtual stranger.

Level 4 - We're more like best friends.

While the emotional connection was limited as Flatmates, at Level 4 we do have a level of closeness and sharing. We're there for each other, and we have goodwill in supporting each other when we are in need. If we see the other person feeling low, we might offer a hug or suggest that we go out for a meal to talk things over. We've perhaps gone through a lot together, and we've seen each other at very low points. There is a sense of mutual concern and thoughtfulness - even a level of love towards our friend.

On the other hand, while we support each other we are still clear that your life is yours, and mine is mine. We might collaborate superficially like watching a TV series that we both love and talking endlessly about why we love it. But we are not overly invested in the path or direction of the other person in more substantial areas of life. We care about our friends, but we can see that each of us has a life direction, and it might well be that those directions bring us to vastly different destinations.

For instance, if one has an exciting opportunity to go and live or work in another country there is a recognition that they will follow the path that is right for them. Sure, we'll keep in touch, and you can call me to check in, we think - but we both know that once we get there, we are going to be building a very different life and meeting lots of new and exciting people.

Friends with "Benefits"

We may decide that as we both happen to be single, that it wouldn't do any harm to meet our sexual needs together for now until something better comes along. We're both fit and healthy after all and we see it consciously or unconsciously as just harmless fun.

"Ok they are definitely not my ideal partner," we think. "But it's something to do, and we get along well so why not?"

It may be that there is an explicit understanding that this is a short-term arrangement, or we may just drift into it - possibly under the influence of alcohol - where it's a kind of fudge. We're not looking to create a life together, and each of us has our own path. Possibly one of the friends would like it to develop into something more, and they consider the sex as a clever way to build and deepen that connection. Something will develop if it's meant to be, they hope.

Does this arrangement lead us towards creating our ideal life with the loving partner that we have dreamed of, or does it provide a kind of obstacle or distraction from creating that life? Are we going to wake up one day and realise that this arrangement has served its purpose for one or both of us? What kind of feelings are going to be present at that point, especially if this is not something that we've explicitly agreed upon?

Level 5 - We're like work colleagues.

Have you ever been part of a well-functioning team at work or in your business where it feels like a well-oiled machine - each person brings qualities to the team and the whole is greater than the sum of its parts? When we have the required skills and the willingness to go the extra mile to support each other to achieve a defined outcome, it's quite incredible what can be achieved!

"People always say what a great unit we are, and how we can overcome anything!", some clients say about their relationship.

When a team is working well, there is a sense that the sum of what is achieved is greater - and sometimes exponentially greater - than what those individuals could achieve individually! Some couples experience this at times of great stress when despite obstacles such as work and financial pressures combined with the requirements of raising children, they can not only survive but to thrive and grow through those experiences. And the relationship strengthens through a sense of joint achievement, so the confidence creates a kind of virtuous cycle.

This can be highly energising and inspiring, and we might well create a life beyond anything that we had imagined was possible - the house, cars, holidays and so on. The kids are thriving too, launched into the world, and making their own magic. However, this does not mean that we necessarily feel emotionally close to our partner. Like with work colleagues though, there is no expectation that we will be vulnerable or connected emotionally to our teammates.

Level 6 - We're co-committed.

Incorporating the benefits of Level 5, at Level 6 we are not only creative in building something greater than the sum of its parts, but we are also emotionally close too. This means that the areas that we can express this creativity are all encompassing - including emotional and spiritual dimensions of our lives, as well as the practical ones.

In his book written along with his wife Marilyn, Irv Yalom shares how she can remember aspects of their life together that he himself is unable to recall[21]. Despite her cancer diagnosis and illness his wife Marilyn still has excellent memory whereas Irv has lost recall of parts of their life despite his overall good health. When they discuss things that they have done together - projects undertaken, books written or travel experiences from earlier in their life Irv may have only limited recall. Marilyn on the other hand can recall details and fill in the spaces, enabling Irv to reconnect with those memories

---

[21] A Matter of Death and Life by Irv Yalom & Marilyn Yalom

and triggering him to remember other related details. In this way she effectively breathes life into Irv's memory and reflection on his life that he wouldn't be able to do alone.

As he considers her approaching death, he reflects on the fact that when she dies elements of his life will effectively die with her. Nobody else would have the experiences and knowledge that Marilyn has on their life together, and with his limited memory this means that those memories and experiences will be effectively lost forever.

On a personal note, my approach tends to be more logical, and acquaintances can comment that I can be someone remote and emotionless. Imagine spending time with a partner like my incredible wife who is more passionate and emotional, and who can awaken some of that quality in me. Would it be possible that when a relationship is really working, we can enable our partners to bring out or express qualities that would otherwise not come to the surface. How could this affect the quality of your life, and the way that you interact and 'ripple into the lives of the people around you'[22]?

---

[22] Phrase taken from the work of Irv Yalom

Relationship Desperation - one more year

Having struggled for years in my own difficult relationship, I'd developed several coping mechanisms in a bid to maintain at least a semblance of normality. I would spend significant periods away using any number of excuses as a great reason to be absent so that I could spend time with people with whom I enjoyed a better relationship. Even when present physically, I had my ways of coping with the difficult atmosphere by being absent emotionally. There were many 'no go areas', where any straying into conversation about those areas would have kicked-off into open or covert war. So, the atmosphere was difficult, and there's no question that I was affected by it on a personal level.

One year I'd sat down with some friends to review my goals for the year, looking at all parts of my life such as fitness, work, parenting, friendship, and relationships. When I looked across the different things that were important to me, I could see that there were several enablers that impacted massively on others, and a key area was my relationship. There was a draining impact on my energy of keeping things going and ensuring that I avoided difficult topics in the interest of keeping the peace.

At that stage I got clear that this was the last year that I was willing to tolerate the costs to myself and the people around me such as my children of perpetuating this toxic situation. There was going to be a solution to this issue one way or another! I also took the step - and the risk - of sharing these goals with my partner to see whether we could work together. It seemed that if we had a sense of joint accomplishment - even in some areas - then perhaps that could help us move forward together.

"Hey, I've been developing my goals for the year, and I was wondering whether you might like to have a read through since there are areas that we could work together on", I suggested.

"Are you listening to me?", she asked. "I don't give a f#@* about your goals... did you get that?"

So thus began my year of (solo!) exploration where I would find out the truth here one way or another. I started to research this topic to get different perspectives on how to make sense of things and to give myself the clarity I was looking for in making sense of this mess in which I found myself. There must be something that I'm doing here that is contributing to this, I thought. Or something that I'm not doing which is keeping me stuck in this cycle of pain.

Part 2 - Reaching the Crossroads

When we can't ignore the problem any more

The challenges that we've looked at so far can go on for some time before we are ready to really take action to resolve them. Often, we develop coping mechanisms to enable us to function to some extent despite the pain and discomfort.

It's like if we've had an injury that hasn't properly healed, and we develop a constant limp in the way we walk. It doesn't look great and feels uncomfortable but since it gets us from A to B, we just get on with it. We're probably struggling and using more energy that we really need to, but it does the job for now.

Then something happens and we just know that something must change. The problem that we've been trying to ignore just can't be ignored anymore and we set our sights on a proper solution rather than just making it through.

Watching my son being bullied

I'd dropped my son off at his sports training and rather than going home and coming back, I took a seat in reception of the sports centre to check some emails while waiting for him. There was space to view through the glass door, so I looked through from time to time to see how he was getting along. I noticed that he was partnered up with another boy and that there was something strange in their interaction.

The other boy kept lifting the ball above his head as if he was going to throw it forcibly at my son, and my son was backing off and cowering away. This developed into a game where my son would retreat to defend himself as the other boy threatened to throw the ball at him. This pattern repeated several times, and I considered entering the hall directly at that point to address the trainer but decided to wait to raise it with my son at the end of the session.

"What was going on there?" I asked. "Why were you letting the other boy intimate you like that?"

"It's no big deal, just a game…" he said.

I was wondering why he was just going along with that behaviour, not standing up for himself or confronting the bullying and intimidation. It just didn't make sense because I saw him as sufficiently assertive in most situations.

Then I had a lightbulb moment.

What was the EXAMPLE that he sees from me repeatedly at home in my own behaviour? If I don't stand up to defend myself against bullying that I'm experiencing myself, why would he learn to do anything different? It's sometimes said that children don't listen much to what we say but never fail to model what we do. And I could see how my own passivity in the face of aggression had not served him but had in fact contributed to an attitude that says that the way to deal with aggression is to roll over and accept it or to pretend that it's not happening.

No shame in getting help.

If our boiler breaks down leading to freezing temperatures in our home, most of us have no issue or shame in reaching out for support. Unless we happen to be an engineer, we know that there is someone better able or qualified to resolve the problem. We might even flirt with the idea of having a go at opening it up ourselves to see what we can find, but then think that the risks or potential downsides mean that it's just not worth it. If we blow up the house, then we've really got an issue!

In the case of our relationship though, the process of recognising that something is broken can take longer. It's not really that bad, we tell ourselves, and in any case, we'll just figure it out somehow. And then there is that nagging feeling of shame that we should just know how to fix things - it can't be that difficult, right?

Getting back to a client in distress

When we receive enquiries from people struggling in their relationships wanting to find out about our services, we always aim to get back to them as quickly as possible. As a mentor once memorably pointed out, some of them are in great difficulty even waking up in the middle of the night crying and not knowing where to turn. The least we can do is to respond to their questions in a prompt way so that they can understand what options are available to them. It may have taken them some considerable time to even summon up the courage to make that inquiry.

"Hi, is that Sarah?" I asked when the phone was answered.

"Ok great, I'm just getting back to you from your inquiry through our website." I continued and introduced myself briefly.

The line suddenly went dead, so I decided to text her so that she could come back to me when she had reception on her phone, or at a better time. A short while later, Sarah did indeed get back to me.

"You won't believe the shame that you've just caused me," she said, obviously agitated and angry. It turned out that she had answered the phone while driving and that there had been others in the car with her at the time. Through the speaker system, they had heard the brief conversation including my introduction.

"Now my children know about my relationship challenges, and I couldn't be more embarrassed," she went on. After giving me a dressing down for being so thoughtless and inconsiderate she made it clear that she would never engage with such an unprofessional service.

Clearly our clients always must make a positive decision to work with us, and they need to consider whether what we do is a good fit for them, for several reasons and considerations! They need to be ready, and we're certainly not looking to persuade anyone! Stepping back, it's worth re-considering the wisdom of answering a call on loudspeaker when we are with others in the car and when you don't know who is calling! It's also worth considering a deeper reality or perspective of what is really going on here.

Firstly, is it *possible* that the moment of this call may NOT have been the first indication to those children that something was not right in this relationship? Could it be that the signs had been there before through daily interactions or through witnessing disagreement. Or could they have been affected by the sour atmosphere that was created. Even if the challenges had been completely hidden behind closed doors, could they have sensed that something is not right. Or even indirectly by picking up on our anxiety or stress in the way that we deal with things?

Additionally, what kind of example do we want to set for our children? Are we someone who ignores our problems, allows them to fester and affect the people around us? Or are we an action taker who gets the support we need to overcome the challenges that we are not able to overcome ourselves?

Which example is a more empowering one, that is going to better serve those children in their lives? Would we want our children to suffer in silence through their challenges or resort to dysfunctional coping strategies and distractions? Or to ignore their challenges, failing to reach their full potential because they decided not to address them?

Surely, we wouldn't want our children to suffer in silence and desperation feeling that their issues are unresolvable. Would we not therefore want to set an example of what it means to take responsibility for getting the help we need to be able to deal with our relationship challenges?

Who is going to look after us when we are old?

While we are young, fit, and strong, the idea that one day we will experience the challenges of ageing and illness may seem like a remote one. It may feel like half a lifetime away and we've got more important things to do in the meantime. But we know on some level that a future is approaching where we may need the love and support from the people around us to maintain our wellbeing.

We could always leave things to chance and look to address our relationship issues when we get to this point of frailty and old age. But is there a chance that we get there and it's more difficult than we anticipated, where the resentment that has set in over the years proves difficult to shift? Our energy levels and focus might be more difficult to summon at that time because of the effects of age on our body and mind. When are we going to have a better opportunity than right now to work to improve things, or to make whatever turns out to be the right decision for us in creating a relationship that works?

Are we able to accept the status quo for the rest of our life?

Could it be that whatever our aspirations or dreams might be for change, that until we make a change that those aspirations won't be realised? Sometimes we might feel that we're stuck in the waiting room of life hoping for something to happen. If we just hang on there, eventually something will turn up, right?

But if we've been waiting there for years, and that train still shows no sign of arriving, are we just going to stay there indefinitely?

"Hmmm, a few people have pointed out that this station closed years ago," we think. "But I'm just going to wait a bit longer JUST IN CASE."

What if we were going to shift and assume that the way things are right now, is going to be the way things remain, unless I act myself to change something? Things are going to remain fundamentally the way they are until I'm ready to own it and put in place some different approaches?

They may come back and re-open that station and our train will finally arrive. But is this really the best strategy to sit there in hope that a miracle may happen? It's sometimes said that the definition of insanity is to continue to do the same things repeatedly and expecting to get a different result.

One more year to D-day?

In my case, it took many years of struggling unhappily before I was ready to make a change. Things had been bad for an awfully long time. We had vastly different ideas in key areas and a level of resentment had set in. There were many no-go areas in terms of conversations that we had tried to have so many times without resolving things that we were walking on eggshells.

"Don't raise these [one of any number of] problems," I might think. "Things are just going to kick off again."

"But hang on, this is important, and it's not going to go away by ignoring it!", I might think.

Not that I had not been looking for help and asking my partner at the time to join me in seeking help to improve things. That was part of the problem, we were both sick of THAT conversation.

"Look, it's not working here, and we need to shift something. It doesn't look like we can do this on our own, or we would have done by now." I might say.

"So go and get help because it seems like you need to work on yourself." she might say.

And I am not blaming anyone else here for the cycle that I was in. It was more my habit of banging my head against a brick wall, and just keeping going regardless that was keeping me in a cycle of despair. I knew that the relationship was not working and that things were happening that were unacceptable and contrary to my values. It was not sustainable in the long term, but surely if I just stuck in there something would eventually change right?

Earlier I mentioned the point where things either changed in my relationship, or that I was going to have to find a solution on my own. If she would join me then great, and I would go all-out to bring her to the table to see whether we might re-find a common vision and shared purpose in building something together. If not, that is ok, but the problem would get addressed one way or another.

At that point it went from being a "nice to have" to being a "must". I quite simply was not willing to perpetuate this madness any longer. No, the costs were too great - not only on myself but for the important people around me.

Assuming makes an "ass" of "u" and "me".

Looking back, I was falling for one of the most common mistakes, in assuming that just because I had a problem that this automatically meant that my partner also had a problem. Surely, we think that if I am struggling with something, then that automatically means that my partner will recognise and want to support me with resolving that problem.

So is this a reasonable assumption or it is possible that our goals and needs could be at odds with one another. What if I am looking to meet my needs of love and connection through the relationship, wanting to be close and emotionally vulnerable with a partner. Does that mean that my partner is necessarily looking to meet that need with me too? She would rather be close to other family members or friends. Is that wrong, or is it in fact up to her?

What if my partner is also invested in the relationship but for other reasons. The needs that she is trying to meet are more practical ones around childcare and financial stability. That the relationship is more of a means to an end in terms of creating a lifestyle through certain kinds of holidays or a quality of life?

What would happen if we just assumed that we are looking to meet the same needs, rather than recognising the true difference of purpose as to why we are there at all?

The most common fears that keep us stuck

When we think of predators, the images that usually come to mind are of the stalking lions closing in on a herd of unsuspecting prey. The lions' agenda is clear, and they have their eyes set on the goal, and the hungry look in their eyes leaves us in no doubt of their intention. The lion is unpretentious in that meat is the only thing on the menu, and it is on the lookout for where the next kill is going to come from!

In addition to non-human animals, can predators also take on human form? Sure, we might say some people also like to hunt. While we may not have the claws and canines of our carnivorous relatives, we have compensated with other instruments from bows and arrows to guns. So sure, humans are also capable of hunting their prey and tracking it down with the same murderous intent as the lion.

But are there other kinds of "hunting", which may not end in a grisly end like the lion's hunt, but have a similar dynamic? How about the door-to-door salesperson targeting older victims with legitimate sounding products or services, or people looking for vulnerable children to exploit in any number of ways. Though these examples may seem remote could it be worth remembering that the possibility of being preyed upon by others remains a possibility? Even despite the risk of us being preyed on by wild animals is far lower than it would have been for our ancestors.

Healthy caution versus all-pervading fear

If real dangers exist in the form of predators - human and non-human - we are surely right and reasonable to have a level of caution as we go about our business.

"Matthew, not everyone is as good hearted as you are," people have sometimes cautioned over the years. While I may have often brazenly shrugged them off there have been situations when they have been right! It can be a form of projection or naivety when we expect others to act with the same level of integrity to which we look to hold ourselves.

On one occasion, I had an initial meeting with a potential business partner to consider a collaboration. I had never met this individual, so it made sense to talk things through and get a feel for each other before taking things any further. The partnership would last a minimum of months, and potentially much longer, and there was a level of financial risk from both sides. On this first meeting, the other person was very polite and plausible in general, though there was one thing that he said that jarred with something he had previously mentioned on the phone. He had previously expressed an interest in "guide dogs", which in our conversation now had developed into "guard dogs".

"Small point", I thought to myself. "It's a strange one, but no big deal."

So, we went ahead with our partnership. And how did things end? Well let us just say that it was a decision I went on to regret!

So, it makes sense to have a level of fear or caution but when taken too far it can affect the quality of our lives.

For instance, for most of us it would make sense to lock our front door at night, before we go to bed! But on the flipside, how about if we take it a step further and barricade our door with furniture every night. Is this a reasonable precaution or could this present other issues. How about if there is a fire or other emergency and we need to get out quickly. Could we have solved a problem but created a bigger problem or risk?

Or how would it affect my life if rather than just locking the door and going to bed, I sit waiting in the dark by the door with a baseball bat, muttering under my breath about what is this country coming to and how we cannot trust anyone nowadays?

What are the most common flavours of fear that come up in our relationship, and how do they affect us when rather than being held in a proper perspective, they become dominant and too influential? Examples of some of the most common variants of fear are:

- Fear of abandonment - that we will be left alone, vulnerable, and lonely.
- Fear of commitment - that we will lose our freedom and feel trapped or constrained.
- Fear of conflict - that we will be in danger if we confront an issue resulting in an argument.
- Fear of losing - that we will be humiliated or ridiculed for a setback or that we will feel shame about ourselves.
- Fear of missing out - that good things are happening, but that they are not available to us.

Putting on our coat of armour

At some point in the past under threat or stress, we have decided that drastic action is needed to maintain our sense of safety from a version of one of these fears. So, we have searched around - lying around at home or sourced online - and found ourselves a coat of armour. A full scale one from the Middle Ages like knights used to wear when they went into battle.

"With this thing on, I'm going to finally feel safe," we say to ourselves as we pull it on for the first time. We look in the mirror and wondering whether it might be over the top, we say to ourselves that at least we are not going to feel vulnerable anymore. And for now, this is the top priority.

We go out in public and sure enough we really do feel protected. While it is heavy and clunky, even if people look at us in surprise, they just don't know how safe it feels in there. In fact, it feels so safe that we are willing to undergo serious discomfort since this is a small price to pay for finally feeling safe. It is bulky but also familiar and even though sleeping in it is challenging, there is no substitute for the sense of certainty and safety that it gives us.

The coat of armour is an analogy to the kinds of coping mechanisms that we adopt to cope with a feeling of unsafety. We keep up a front so that nobody sees our emotions or how we are affected by things. If people, see us as tough and uncompromising they are going to know not to mess with us. Or we find a way to distract or intoxicate ourselves from facing those difficult emotions head on.

Time to take it off?

We have worn that coat of armour for years, and we've become familiar with it. We have even found a position of sleep that makes it just about possible to have a decent night's rest. It may be getting smelly inside after all these years, but a quick spray of deodorant every morning still does the trick, and in any case, we are used to the smell by now.

We have had moments of doubt for sure, as we've seen people through the visor that seem to be enjoying themselves much more than us and living a full and healthy life without the armour. That day on the beach maybe when we saw other parents running around and playing with the kids, jumping in the sea, and enjoying an ice cream. But even though our kids wanted to play we just could not face a game of beach ball wearing the armour. That was just too much, so we had to say no. And we really fancied an ice cream, but it made such a mess on that visor.

Or at the dance class where we were trying to learn salsa with our partner, and there was no escaping the feeling that we would be having much more fun without the armour. Sure, we still have some movement, but it was so difficult to move to the music and to feel our partner's movement and energy through the armour.

Then one day, it reaches a point where we can no longer deny that while the armour served a purpose at some point in the past, it is just not something compatible with the quality of life that we want to experience. It is time with all our love and honour in the world, to put the armour into retirement and to experience the freedom and joy that we know is available to us. Even though people are going to see us in a way that we have not allowed them to for a while, we know that the price we have paid until today or wearing it, is not something we are willing to pay for the rest of our lives.

Part 3 - A path towards Clarity

Once we have accepted that change is not only necessary but essential, and that we're not willing to accept the price that inaction has cost us in the past, we take a step forward. We may not yet know exactly what we need to do, but we are clear that something must change. It may be a tentative step at first, feeling our way and still not really knowing what our solution is going to be.

Even so, this can be a moment of substantial relief to know that we are committed to a solution, whatever that solution may be. We are now committed to action and movement, and it is important to honour that part of us which has come to see something more clearly.

Becoming Conscious of What we want

What is the difference between going shopping with a list versus just turning up and wondering about until our trolley is full? Could it be that we get distracted by this or that shiny object or exclusive offer and that when we come to review at home, we have missed some essentials? We get the short-term excitement of trying this or that novelty but then run short of what we really needed later in the week or must make an extra unscheduled trip.

For bigger purchases the stakes are even higher. If you walk into a car showroom without any research or forethought as to what you are looking for is there any potential danger? You see a car that really stands out to you for its size or prestige, or the salesman presents you with an unmissable offer available for a short time only. The only issue is that it was not what you really needed.

Is there a decision that is going to affect the quality of our life and our outcomes in the long term other than choosing our partner, or a decision about whether we want to stay in a relationship? Could there be any value in getting clear about what we want or do not want before we enter the "showroom". If we do not get clear, could another shiny object distract us, only to review it later at home and wonder what we have done? Could we have made a clearer or more refined decision by being conscious about what we were looking for and what is important to us. How would this have enabled us in making the right decision or to be able to move towards the right relationship for us?

Getting the rock moving

Imagine that you have the task of moving a substantial rock from A to B. You have the support of others and favourable conditions as you've got a downward slope to help you! On the other hand, you have still got to get the boulder moving and it looks like it might have been stuck there for a while. It is going to take some energy to move it, but at least once it's rolling, we should be able to keep it going. And then once it has got some momentum it should just roll on down the hill all the way to its destination.

Our path of change can be like the rock. It can take some work to get it moving and we might need some help at the start. But once we have some movement, we will have forward momentum and we can build on that from there. Also, once we see some change, we will be feeling brighter and already have a sense of achievement that we are on our way!

The problem with some relationship therapy

"How has your week gone?" the counsellor asks.

"Not great, we had a big bust up on Monday", the client responds and goes on to give their side of the story as the other partner listens impatiently waiting to have their turn, pretending to listen but inwardly fuming.

"Yeah, that's one side of the story… here's mine", says the other partner, as they describe the counter argument and what they really think was going on. They then get into an uncomfortable back and forth that feels terribly like what happens at home, only with the added embarrassment that a third party must witness this.

The counsellor does their best to keep the conversation as calm as possible, containing everyone at least until the end of the hour when they go home. "Job done, at least for another week," thinks the counsellor. How do the clients feel having simply come and re-heated another frustrating argument that seemed to lead nowhere?

"How long are we going to do this for?", they eventually reflect on it as they consider themselves going around in circles again.

Talking is useful though, right?

Well, in two words, "It depends."

Because we may be simply talking about the symptom of the problem. Using the analogy from earlier, this means that we might be discussing the best design of wallpaper to paste over the crack in the wall. We can talk about THAT question all day long even in the calmest and considered way and still not be ANY closer to a solution for the underlying problem in the foundations of our house!

So, it is truer to say that a CERTAIN type of talking is useful, and it's the type that is focussed on identifying or addressing the underlying causes of the challenge that we are experiencing. This is what we do in our work with couples and individuals, and this section is going to reveal some of the key principles that we need to understand to do so!

Breakthrough 1 - Is my relationship a safe place?

As we have looked at earlier, the mechanisms that we employ to establish safety if we are feeling unsafe, are likely to limit the success of our relationship. We naturally erect barriers, but it is very difficult to have a great relationship with someone standing behind a barrier!

So how can we address safety in a more functional way, that sets the foundations for a healthy relationship?

Self-awareness

Sometimes we may clearly see how we have come into a defensive mindset (standing behind the barrier), and what was the specific lack of safety that led us to that point. At other times we might simply experience the effects of this mindset, through distancing, reactivity, or anxiety. To get a better perspective on what is really happening for us, it is essential that we find a way to keep a proper perspective.

Standing on the bridge

One metaphor used to help us picture this sense of perspective, is to picture ourselves standing on a bridge overlooking a river[23]. Imagine that you are looking down on that river from far above observing what is going on.

---

[23] Lair Torrent, The Practice of Love

"Wow, there's a lot of water in there… sure, we've had some heavy rain recently", we might think.

"Hey, there's a lot of people around… maybe there's a party or an event going on later."

Whatever we observe from the bridge, we can reflect and consider with some perspective. I will go down there myself and join in, we might wonder. Or we may decide to stay on the bridge for longer, observing and reflecting.

Versus being IN the water!

An alternative perspective on the river could be gained by dropping down from the bridge and getting IN the river. You would certainly get an up close and personal view of what is going on, and at certain times that might be desirable or enjoyable.

But would you be able to have the same perspective on the situation from being in the water, as you are able to have when you are on the bridge? Could there be other things taking up your attention - like fighting for your life, or getting ourselves out as quickly as possible - when you find yourself in the water?

When we're in the water in our relationship?

How do these different perspectives play out in our relationship? Does our ability to maintain an objective perspective change the way that we relate to the people around us? At the times that we find ourselves in the river in our relationship - fighting for our preservation - could we even do or say things that we regret or that cause damage?

When we are unable to remain 'on the bridge' in our relationship, one of the consequences is that we quickly become overly and unhealthily reactive. Rather than being able to pause to consider the correct response we will find ourselves 'triggered' into a comment or reaction which we may then come to regret - either immediately or subsequently. Like when we feel that we are drowning we will reach for anything that comes to hand in the river that might enable us to reach safety.

The reason that we focus on this as a key ingredient with our work with couples is that until we can catch ourselves in this way, it's virtually impossible to consistently apply anything else that we learn.

The power of mindfulness

Over the last two decades mindfulness and meditation have been extensively studied from a scientific perspective. Even as recently as the early 2000s, these disciplines occupied a more 'alternative' place in many people's understanding, conjuring pictures of remote monks sitting in rooms full of incense and candles. For many of us, there seemed little fit with our contemporary lives.

Substantial scientific work has since been undertaken, with major academic institutions setting up whole departments looking at the impact and potential benefits of these disciplines. Stanford University for instance is host to the "Center for Compassion and Altruism Research and Education" which provides many resources, including peer-reviewed articles[24].

For instance, neuroimaging scans of people undertaking meditation have shown deep and lasting changes to the way the brain works because of undertaking meditation practices. Meditation has been shown to activate brain areas involved in processing self-relevant information, self-regulation, focussed problem solving, adaptive behaviour as well as improving self-awareness[25]. These benefits have been reported for centuries by the people who practise them, and now science has caught up and shown us how this really works.

Emerging from a very dark place

In my early 20s I found myself in a very dark place in my life. I may have appeared to others like I was doing well with a respectable job, friends and outwardly confident, but inside I was a mess. I was riven with inner conflict as I tried to digest the different ideas and values that I saw in the world around me. Having gone through a university education while also taking on board many of

---

[24] http://ccare.stanford.edu/research/peer-reviewed-ccare-articles/

[25] https://www.ncbi.nlm.nih.gov/pmc/articles/PMC4471247/

the ideas and goals that are taken by a given in the world around me, I was struggling to find any worthwhile purpose or meaning for myself.

"Is this really all there is to it", I thought. "I just need to work to try to rise above all these other people to have the best house or car. And then one day I might retire and put my feet up for a while until I die?"

It felt like something was missing, and I knew that I wanted more. I was unhappy, but I was also searching for something to help me make sense of all these difficult emotions and confusion. And my habits weren't helping but were rather holding me back from finding any clarity. The alcohol that I was consuming may have numbed the pain and confusion for a while but did little to progress me towards a solution.

During this search I stumbled upon meditation! At that stage, it was almost unbearable to just sit at home in my own company so I was always on the lookout for mid-week activities that I could join to keep me occupied! On my local high street, I saw a poster for a drop-in beginner's meditation, and I thought why not. It's on an evening when I'm free, and who knows maybe I'm going to learn something.

"Well, I know I'm stressed," I thought. "Maybe this can help me calm down a bit."

"Also, who knows, maybe I'm going to meet some cool alternative types that I can impress with my achievements and my life."

From the very first session I knew that I was onto something that had the potential to really help me shift to a different place and to get myself together. I also found myself inspired and curious about the people I met there - they were so calm, happy, and focussed even with what looked like very simple lives.

"That's incredible," I thought. "Is that even possible?"

Looking back, the impact of those friends was a key factor in my ability to stand back from the conveyor belt that I felt that I was on and to find a new path to navigate. It showed that while it may take some time to fully manifest that there was at least a viable dream to hold on to.

Happiness versus Fulfilment

The kind of happiness that I was looking for in those days was a very fragile and provisional one. It depended on getting a certain outcome or result or having the approval of people whose opinion I valued. While these results might lead to some short-term feelings of relief, they failed to yield any real meaning or satisfaction. Was there something deeper, I wondered that rather than giving me a quick fix of relief gave me a longer-term sense that I was on the right path and living a meaningful life?

Being Safe versus FEELING safe - putting mindfulness to work in our relationship.

It's one thing to objectively know that we are safe. We may know that we are safe in our home, we have food in the fridge and the heating is on. However, we can be objectively safe, but still FEEL unsafe, and this feeling can impact on the way we show up with our partner. It is therefore important to become more self-aware, and to learn how to calm ourselves with the parasympathetic nervous system using the breath, by slowing, deepening, and lengthening the outbreath helping us to regulate our heart rate. Once practised, this can quickly lead us to feeling more grounded and secure in the moment and less likely to react in dysfunctional ways.

Are healthy boundaries in place?

There are many ways of thinking about what acceptable and unacceptable behaviour is, but how do we cut through this and really understand where the correct lines should be drawn. We may have an uncomfortable feeling that something may not be right, but how do we get underneath a gut feeling to really see the truth? I might be walking down the street with a gut feeling that the bogeyman (or "bogeyperson") is about to jump out and attack me, only to realise that the film I was watching the previous night had a remarkably similar looking scene!

Sure, tread carefully but also remember that we experience our own reality which is influenced by our conditioning. It doesn't necessarily mean that it's true on some ultimate level. Do dark corners exist in the world without a bogeyperson lurking around them?

Following our intuition

Have you ever had a gut feeling about a situation or person that you just couldn't shake. You can't put your finger on what exactly it is that doesn't ring true, but you know that something isn't right? How about when you've ignored this feeling and proceeded regardless? Has that ever led you into challenging situations?

Intuition has its limitations!

In his book Thinking Fast and Slow, author Daniel Kahneman shows how we are prone to buying into stories and narratives that we might "intuitively" believe are correct but that can systematically be shown to be wrong. If we can latch onto a reasonable looking narrative, we can lose the correct perspective and make decisions which we may come to reflect do not make any sense at all.

For example, experiment participants in an experiment were shown to attach a higher probability to:

1. "Roger Federer lost the first set but then went onto win the match", than to the proposition that:

2. "Roger Federer lost the first set".

"Yes, my intuition is telling me that must be right, because Roger is a legend so I'm sure he goes on to win the match," we think.

The problem is that every instance of the first proposition is WITHIN the second one. This means that even if he had lost the first AND lost the match only once, there would still be more instances of the second statement being true. This has happened many times during Roger's career, even though he is a legend, he can't win every time! Because it doesn't have the same ring to it, we are drawn towards the former statement.

This is an example of where we need to be wary of that 'gut feeling' or intuition - the "fast" thinking - because we know how easy it is to buy into a narrative which could also be a simple stereotype or discriminatory. In this example, the "slow" thinking is the statistical understanding described that the first statement is WITHIN the second one. And while there is no ultimate "right" way of thinking, Kahneman argues that we systematically make these kinds of mistakes when going with our "gut feeling".

Oversimplifying "Bad behaviour"

We might have a sense or gut feeling that our partner is misbehaving, but does that mean that boundaries are being breached, leading to something that can be objectively and legitimately considered to be a kind of "abuse"? It's one thing to recognise our feelings, and true enough that if we feel something then that is indeed our feeling, and true for us.

"I feel that my partner is disrespectful and abusing me," we might say. That is a useful reflection to a point and may well be indicating a deeper truth. There can certainly be value in speaking our truth and feeling heard though we need to maintain some perspective and clarity, especially when it comes to potentially making accusations towards others.

An example could be when on examination or through discussion the uncomfortable feeling is that we don't like our partner going out with their friends because we find ourselves suffering anxiety of other people looking at them or having conversations with them. But can we then say that our partner choosing to go out with her friends really constitutes "bad behaviour" or "abuse" on their part towards us? Are we therefore the victim of abuse?

"No, they have never been unfaithful to my knowledge," we think. "But they are really attractive, so you never know."

So, the question is whether just because we feel anxious or uncomfortable, does that mean that our partner is breaching a boundary in some way or doing something "wrong"? Again, we need to take a step beyond just a feeling or intuition that something isn't right and look to make sense of things with a more rational framework.

An Alternative Model - My Business, Your Business and God's Business

Developed from the work of Byron Katie[26] let's consider an alternative way of understanding boundaries and how we can make sense of them to understand what relationship abuse really looks like.

"My business"

With the concept of "My business" we are looking to identify things that naturally sit within my remit or frame of decision making. This would include how we choose to behave or act, as well as how we respond or speak to others. It also includes our own emotions or feelings, as well as any work we choose to do on ourselves such as attending a course or reading this book. It would also include things as simple as what I decide to have for breakfast to the work I choose to do and any agreements I choose to enter like a relationship or marriage. Similarly, if I decide to enter into a future agreement or to end such an agreement, it would also be "my business".

---

[26] Loving What Is by Byron Katie

"Your business"

In the context of our relationship (or any relationship), we can consider "your business" to be that which relates to our partner. So, using the same thinking as above, this is everything that sits naturally in the remit of our partner. Their behaviour and how they choose to react and communicate with other people would be included, for instance. Again, our partner's feelings, beliefs, and priorities are their business. What they choose to do for a living, what they have for breakfast and their decision to work on themselves or to read any book such as this one. Also, any commitments that they choose to enter such as a contract - whether in relationships or any other domain of life - is their business. And again, their decision to commit to a relationship with us or with anyone else - or to end that commitment - is also their business.

"God's business"

Whether or not we believe in God in a religious sense or not, the idea of "God's business" is that sense that some things are simply beyond our control. We could also think of them being in the "hands of the universe" if we prefer. Either way, we're looking to include the things in our life that we simply have to accept.

For example, if we've planned a barbecue but the weather isn't supportive, can we really influence that? Or our business is affected by a wider political or economic factor such a recession or pandemic - again, is outside of our control. We simply must adapt ourselves to that reality.

"It shouldn't be raining", sounds like an absurd statement but how easy is it to feel like the victim of unfortunate circumstances like the thunderstorm on the day of our parade.

As the rain in this example is "God's business", this would be a simple example of a breach of boundary in the model. We are trying to control or influence something that we cannot. And how do we feel when we say or think such a statement, empowered or disempowered?

On the flipside, when we step back into "My business" and think what I can do about this, maybe we realise that there is an indoor alternative to the barbecue that we had planned and while it's not the same as what we'd hoped for, we can still have fun! Because we can make this decision - even if it requires hiring another venue - this then falls back into the remit of 'My business". And how do we then feel when we take back control and step into a decision that we can make?

So far, so simple, right?

When boundaries break down

So how do boundaries break down in relationships, and how does this help us to get a clearer and more objective view of what constitutes "bad behaviour", beyond the challenges of just relying on a feeling that "I'm not happy with what my partner is doing"?

"If you don't do x, watch out!"

The first category of boundary breaches is when we encounter a direct threat or consequence of not complying with a request. Imagine two people facing off in a confrontation where an explicit threat is made.

"If you go out with your friends, then your clothes are going to be out on the street when you get back", someone might say.

How a person chooses to spend their time is their business. We could certainly have a conversation and state our opinion - that is our business.

"Do you know, it would be helpful if you could stay in tonight because I've got a lot of work to finish, and I haven't got the headspace to also watch the kids. Would that be ok?", we might ask. So far, so good. We have a point of view, and we state it to our partner - both of which are OUR business.

However, whether our partner chooses to agree to our request or not is whose business?

"No, they should do what I say", we might think or say.

This would be a breach of boundary because what they choose to do is their business not ours!

If we then engage in a threat like in the example above this would be an instance of overt aggression as we are stepping over their boundary and controlling something that naturally sits within their remit.

"If you go out, I'm going to punch you in the face", could be an even more extreme example in this case. Again, at this point we're using a threat to control something that is not our business. This kind of statement is the first - and most visible and obvious - example of abuse.

"If you do x, which means that you don't really love me".

The second category of abuse to consider is where the breach of boundary has a more emotional component. The words may not be stated in exactly this form, but there is a clear sense that in saying that by behaving a certain way, shows that you don't care about me or love me.

Let's take an example.

One partner had decided to have a glass of wine on a particular evening and was settling down to watch TV - her time, her decision, her body... her business!

"I'm having some wine, would you like to join me?",
again an invitation which is her business.

"No thanks, I'll join you later to watch some TV, but I've
got a few things to finish and, I've got an early start and
a long drive, so I need a clear head. So thanks, but no
thanks."
So far, so good. She has made an invitation which is her
business. And he has responded, which is his business.

"So you'll have a drink with your friends, but you won't
drink with me," she then responds.

Can you hear a version here, of "you don't really love
me", or at least "it seems that you don't love me as
much as you love your friends", because otherwise why
would you not want to have a drink with me. What is
going on with this statement, or what is she trying to
achieve with this statement?

If we start by saying that whether he accepts her
invitation to drink or not is HIS business, what is she
doing when she makes this statement? Firstly, in trying
to force or guilt-trip him into joining her for a drink this is
a breach of boundary because she's stepping into his
business. In addition, whether he loves her or not - or
whether he has any feeling or emotion about anything
for that matter - is his business.

So as soon as we step in and TELL someone that we
are going to interpret their decision to do or not do

something as meaning that they don't love us, it is a breach of boundary. Our feelings are OURS to determine and it is not for other people to tell us how we feel!

It may be coming from a good place...

In this example, the woman who is overstepping boundaries simply wants to connect with her partner and spend some quality time together. It's not coming from a place of being nasty or unkind. But how easily we can find ourselves stepping over a boundary even with what feels to us like a positive intention!

It may seem like too harsh a word to use for this kind of behaviour, but we are talking about a level of relationship ABUSE when we identify any breaches of boundaries. How does it make us feel when we have a sense that our boundaries are being overstepped in this way?

Natural Consequences

"She shouldn't have said that" we might then think to ourselves.

But what she says or doesn't say is whose business? This statement is also a breach of boundaries as we are getting involved in something - the words that come out of her mouth - that we simply cannot control!

On the other hand, what COULD we control to stay within the guidelines of "My business". Well as well as choosing to read this book, you could take the next step and say that we need to get help to work on things and get us out of this negative cycle that we are in.

Our decision to stay in a relationship with someone is our business. So, if the situation gets to a point where we feel that it can't be improved or worked upon, we may have a decision to make.

"No, I've got to stay for the kids", is also a breach of boundaries because it's making a decision which is "My business", someone else's decision. In this case the someone is a vague sense of something imposed by another entity which we may or may not have determined, so therefore we could say that we're making "my business", "god's business".

Where the law can be more challenging

We've looked at two different types of breaches of boundary, and it's worth reflecting on how the law of the land would impact on each of these situations.

"Officer, you need to come around because my partner is saying that he'll punch me in the face if I go out with my friends", you might ask the emergency operator.

In the case of an overt threat - especially to our physical wellbeing - there is a good chance that the police will respond quickly. If it is us making the threat - whatever our gender - we could well expect to be explaining ourselves to law enforcement soon.

How about in the second case?

"Officer, you need to come around because my partner is trying to get me to have a glass of wine, and I've said no but she's quite insistent..." we might ask the police operator.

"No, I've already told her, but now she's saying that it means I don't love her", we keep going.

"What do you mean you can't help, this is a clear breach of boundaries because my feelings are my business, right?"

While there have been laws in the UK in the areas of coercive control since 2015, it's at least possible that we might find this conversation more challenging than in the first case!

The importance of correct boundaries in our relationship

Putting aside any legal considerations, it's important to note that in our model that both overt aggression and covert aggression are breaches of boundaries and forms of abuse. While they may be subject to different laws, in terms of the "natural laws" of our relationship they will both lead us into a mess, if we are intending to experience a loving relationship.

It's critical that we identify and reassert correct boundaries because we find that whatever other good qualities, we might have that when the boundaries are breached, this will ALWAYS lead to a level of negativity and resentment. This may come out immediately in a negative reaction, or it may fester then eventually come out into the open in an unexpected way when we least wanted it. Either way, until we identify and resolve these boundaries, we can guarantee that our relationship will feel unstable and unsafe.

Can we accept our partner the way they are?

Let's say that our partner is struggling with a problem, and they ask for help. It could be something simple and practical or even something more emotional or involved.

"Look I'm really struggling at work and finding myself stressed and angry so much of the time and I'm worried it's impacting on other areas," they might say.

In this sense the driver for change has come from our partner, in reaching out for support. At this stage, if we care for the person we might well decide to help in some way if we are able to. It could be that we go into listening mode to give emotional support, or to give them a hug and let them know that we are there for them. At other times, the help requested might be more practical, in researching resources or a book that could be useful to them.

And if we do support, how would that impact our relationship with that person? Could our bond with them be strengthened by that sense of care and taking the time to help at a moment of need?

When we are driving the change

How about if the person is NOT asking for help, but that we ourselves are identifying the problem area for which that person requires support?

"No, it's just that I want him to be the best version of himself," we might hear. "I can see that he's struggling, and he'll be happier that way."

Are there any hidden challenges here that could impact our relationship? Even when we feel that we are coming from a good place, could there be any unintended consequences of proposing or imposing a solution on someone who is not asking for support?

Imagine that you are walking happily down the street, and someone approaches you to offer you a crutch.

"Oh no, thanks," you say. "I'm absolutely fine!"

But then a few minutes later you are again offered the crutch, and this time you decline again but start to think that something weird is going on here! How about if by the time you arrive at your destination lots of people

164

have offered you a crutch? How long would it take before you start to wonder if they've seen something that you don't recognise yet, and maybe you do need the crutch after all.

"Ok, maybe you're right," we might eventually say. "Let me try the crutch for a while and see how it goes."

Could it even be that through the power of belief that you adapt your walking style and before long you really do find it difficult to walk without the crutch?

"Hey, they were right, this crutch feels pretty comfortable now."

For whose benefit is the crutch?

In this sense, even though we see the crutch as being useful for the other person, who are we really trying to help when we offer that crutch? The other person may be struggling but they may also be happy to continue struggling in that way. Or they may not have a problem at all from their perspective.

So, could it be that the issue is really with us observing uncomfortably, wanting to reassure ourselves or comfort ourselves with a sense that we are helping the other person? And let's say the person does accept the crutch and limps on, and we then feel better having supported them. Have we really helped the other person, or have

we more accurately helped someone else closer to
home?

Radical acceptance of our partner

This issue comes up regularly where there is something
about our partner that we find uncomfortable or even
intolerable to observe. They look stressed, or we see
them repeatedly losing their temper or shouting for
example. It could be that we feel the effects of that
behaviour directly on ourselves, or more indirectly
through observation.

If we were to really accept them the way they are, would
that have an impact on us? We know deep down that
the current situation is not viable in the long term, and
we fear the consequences of ending the relationship.
What would happen to the house, who would look after
the kids and where would I even live, we might ask
ourselves.

The simple though often difficult reality is that we can
only assume that our partner is going to stay exactly the
way they are for the rest of their lives. Sure, they might
at some point decide to make a change. But that
decision rests purely with themselves.

Because the impact of being with a partner while holding
the expectation that they will change is guaranteed to
have a negative effect on the relationship, and
especially on their sense of feeling loved. It's just not

possible for that weight of expectation to be completely invisible to our partner over time, whether through our tonality or even disapproving looks.

My own journey towards acceptance

In my own previous failing relationship, I struggled for years in accepting certain qualities and behaviours in my partner. Why does she never greet me when I try to give her a hug, and why does she never smile and share in my successes or accomplishments, I wondered. Why does nothing I do ever seem to be enough, but that I feel criticised for falling short of some undefined standard? How is it that she's so lovely and nice towards her friends and other family members, but when it comes to me, I feel so rejected and ignored?

This then led me to proposing lots of solutions that I thought might help, whether it be suggesting that we go to counselling together, or to recommend a book or a magazine article. I would have certainly said at that time that the change I was looking for was for her benefit, although clearly, I was also seeing advantages for myself and the other people around us if she could "correct" those challenges.

After having turned down support several times, how could my repeated invitations have impacted on the relationship, or to have made her feel? Did she even have a problem from her own perspective? Well, she certainly wasn't asking for help or looking for help, so what could have been a better approach?

It was me that had the problem all along, and that I was simply looking to solve that problem by changing her? Whose business is it whether she decides or wants to change, in any case?

Taking the model we looked at earlier, what would have been a better focus in terms of staying within 'my business'? Well, I'd certainly asked her to address certain things that I'd struggled with and making that request in a respectful way is certainly within my remit. But she had turned down that invitation multiple times so where do I go from here?

Eventually I came to see that while her behaviour was her business, I still had a crucial decision to make for myself. Because staying in a relationship with someone is always our business, and I was paying the price not of her behaviour but of my own decision to stay in this toxic dynamic. And that this toxicity was being at least partially created by the sense that I was conveying that she was unacceptable to me the way she was.

So, is it more loving to stay with a partner resentfully trying to change them, or to accept them the way they are while also deciding that the relationship is no longer viable?

Examining and re-establishing "Integrity"

While we each have our own understanding of morality and correct behaviour, there are some recurring or timeless principles worth considering and reflecting on. In some cases, there may be disagreement over whether a certain principle is valid, where we have a substantial difference in understanding a core idea.

More often, the differences are in how we apply a certain principle and whether it correctly links to a certain behaviour or situation. For example, we might agree that to communicate truthfully is a good thing but disagree on exactly how this principle applies to a given situation. Or you might say that another principle such as non-harm overrides truthfulness in a certain context.

You will recognise many of the principles here, and in some cases, they are backed up by national law and in other cases they may be partially in line with the legal system. It could be that laws are only applicable in certain instances but that a kind of moral law applies to other situations. We might instantly sense that something is 'wrong' even when no law applies at all. There may also be aspects reflected in spiritual or religious guidelines.

Avoiding inflicting "harm" on our partner

If we have any sense that our partner is liable to harm us, we are highly likely to react in some way to keep ourselves safe from that harm or potential harm. Once we retreat or cut ourselves off to defend ourselves, it's extremely unlikely that our relationship will be a strong and loving one. We may even at some point - either consciously or unconsciously - find ourselves retaliating and thinking,

"Well, if she's going to push my buttons in this area, maybe I'll push hers in another."

It's therefore crucial that we identify and minimise - if not eliminate - any areas where we are inflicting any kind of harm on our partner. In some cases of "gross" harm, this might be quite easy to identify. We know that our partner is very defensive towards his parents, so we know that pointing at their challenges will create a reaction.

"There you go again," we say. "Just like your dad!" as we enjoy seeing the frustration and rage building up in them.

"That'll teach him to challenge me in that way!" we think.

In other cases, the harm can be more subtle, and we need to access a deeper level of self-honesty to really come to terms with it. We like to tell ourselves that we did the right thing but that if we're honest with ourselves there was some aspect of wanting to prove a point or teach our partner a lesson.

A personal example would be a home decorating project that we undertook to re-paint a room in our house. The idea to change the colour scheme had come from my wife, and while I could see that she really wanted to do it, there was part of me thinking that the current paint job was perfectly adequate and functional! It "does the job", I thought!

Seeing how important this was to her, I recognised that it would really make an enormous difference to how she felt in that room and that a coat of paint isn't the greatest cost in the world after all!

However, I also knew how busy we were with our different projects, so I built in a small lesson into the work. It was only afterwards that I was conscious of this, and at the time it was just the faintest of thoughts that briefly crossed my mind.

Ok, I thought, this is going to be more time consuming than you think so rather than getting the decorators in, we are going to do it ourselves and we'll see how much time we spend not only painting, but covering things, moving things and so on. This will make you think twice next time!

Having recognised this negative mindset later, I was able to name it and own it. We reflected on how easily these agendas can play out, even though the activity of supporting our partner with something that is important to them. We may well be 'helping', but is there some other underlying agenda that we are throwing into the mix at the same time?

Not taking what isn't given.

Do we ever have a feeling that something of ours has been taken without our agreement? Do we maintain the same level of respect with our partner's things as we would with a friend, colleague, or someone we don't know. Sometimes in our relationship we can get lazy and think to ourselves that our partner's stuff is really ours, and vice versa.

"It was only a phone charger, after all," we might reason.

But if our partner is running late to leave the house, and they really need that charger and they are sure that they left it in the same place and then the reason it's not there turns out to be us, how are they going to feel? At this point, it's no longer really about the phone charger, but more about a level of respect for each other that could easily lead to resentment.

Or if we've asked for a couple of hours of space to finish an important project, and that we only want to be disturbed in an emergency but then we are interrupted because they want to tell us about this great television programme, how might we feel. It's connected again to boundaries and respect, and that if we feel that we are respected ourselves are we more or less likely to return that level of respect to the other person?

An unexpected arrival

A client had understood that his wife was still taking her birth control medication when she announced that she was pregnant with their third child. It turned out that she had unilaterally decided to stop taking the tablets as she'd found that her sister was pregnant and thought that it would be good to have playmates of the same age when the children were born. How mixed the feeling could have been when the thought of a new arrival to the family is tainted by a sense of betrayal of something taken that wasn't explicitly given. In this case the agreement to have a new addition to the family is the aspect that was taken, leaving a sense of 'theft' even though in this case the law may give little support.

Speaking the truth

How many times do we need to know that our partner is telling a lie for us to start to doubt everything that they are saying? Isn't it true that trust takes time to establish that it can be damaged in the blink of an eye? If we lose that sense of trust in our partner, how is that going to play out in the relationship? If you are playing a team sport and the team members lose confidence or belief in each other, are they going to be able to work as a well-functioning team?

"It wasn't a lie, I just decided not to share that detail with you," we might reason. But if the detail omitted is something that we know would have been important to the other person, are we still in integrity by not letting them know. How is it going to impact our level of trust when that fact becomes known later?

Avoiding Sexual Misconduct

Could there be any potential downsides to engaging in sexual activity where there isn't any positive emotional connection? Let's say that the relationship isn't working, but that sex becomes a form of distraction away from resolving those problems. Does that take us towards a solution to the issue, or is it a form of staying stuck and going around in circles?

What about if our sexual relationship is more recreational or about having fun? Is this harmless or could there be unintended consequences that could impact on ourselves and others. Even beyond unwanted pregnancies or sexually transmitted diseases, could we find ourselves building a level of connection with someone who is unsuitable as a partner. If we want to have a longer-term relationship, does this take us towards that goal or is it a distraction away from achieving the kind of relationship that is going to serve us?

"No, it's ok, over time they are going to GROW to like me and then we'll have a proper relationship," we might hope. But does "living in hope" sound like a good strategy when the person has made no indication that this is what they want?

Avoiding Intoxication

Have you ever done anything that you regret while intoxicated? If we want to maintain a high level of integrity around our behaviour, would it be helpful to avoid consuming or engaging in anything that puts us in a state of intoxication?

One of my earliest relationships ended through my own bad behaviour while intoxicated, and this was a harsh lesson. There was nowhere to turn and nobody else to blame but myself and it led me to reevaluate my relationship with alcohol. There was such an imbalance between the pain that was caused through this indiscretion and the level of enjoyment or happiness in the drunken act. I couldn't even properly remember what happened - what a mess!

On top of that, three of my peers died as teenagers under the influence of alcohol. One drowned while on holiday having decided to take a late-night swim, not having seen the warning signs of currents. Another choked on his own vomit after sitting back and dozing off after one too many during a night of drinking with friends. Yet another decided that it would be a clever idea to take a drive in his car after drinking and paid the price with his life.

In each case, I've always wondered whether there was a moment of realisation or clarity when they each knew that this was the end, where they asked themselves whether this drunken adventure was worth it. What dreams did they forsake and what could they have achieved or experienced in their lives had they lived to tell the tale. Are we heading in the same direction, or are we able to heed their lesson before it's too late in our case?

Breakthrough 2 - Communication paths are open.

Once we've established that the basic principles of safety are in place, we can dive into some specifics around how to fix our broken communication. If we are unable to communicate effectively, we may stop trying from which point it's very difficult to build the relationship back to where we want it to be.

Dancing with our partner

We've used the analogy of the dance throughout this book, as a way of thinking about the quality and dynamic of our relationship. As soon as we consider that we are dancing together with our partner, whether we have initiated the dance or whether we've accepted the offer of dancing, there are some important dynamics that come into play.

When a dance is choreographed, both partners take instruction and leadership from the choreographer. This can be like some relationship therapy where the therapist is instructing the clients how to dance, and it can create a beautiful dance - at least in the short term. On the other hand, a different kind of teacher is giving us the understanding and techniques to be able to dance spontaneously ourselves. This means that when we find ourselves on the dancefloor of our life we can adapt and flow and make the dance work, even when we don't know exactly what song is going to come on next.

So, the type of dancing we are considering is non-choreographed couples dancing such as salsa, bachata, ceilidh and so on.

Also, it is worth remembering that even for a person who loves dancing more than anything else, there will be times when we are not dancing! For instance, when we are putting out the bins or doing the grocery shopping the fact that we love dancing doesn't really come into play. Or we are thinking or dreaming about the next time we can dance with our partner. In any case, the analogy only plays out for the time we choose to dance.

Why does the dance matter anyway?

There are several ways that we can approach the dancing which we can GUARANTEE are not going to work, and it's a helpful image to consider. Imagine for instance that BOTH partners decide to be the leader of the dance at the same time. Is that ever going to be a beautiful, inspiring, attractive dance or not? How much fun are those two people going to be having? For how long are they going to keep up the efforts of maintaining the dance, and could they even harm each other during the process?

Coming back to our sphere of relationships, would such a dynamic be sustainable or viable in the long term? At some point, the topic of today's disagreement is not even important. Today's clash could be about a holiday and tomorrow could be about where we're going shopping. For as long as this dynamic is playing out things are always going to have that underlying tension and conflict! You might have two people that are individually very respectful and loving but if this dynamic is at play, the relationship could feel like an uncomfortable place to be!

A word about gender

The dancing analogy can be triggering for some people as a typical image of a couple dancing could be a man and woman dancing together with the man leading and the woman following. However, the issue described where the dance breaks down with both partners trying to lead applies to any gender combination. It could be two men, two women, two non-binary identifying individuals or a man and a woman and the clash would have a similar quality.

Understanding masculinity and femininity

If gender is not the driving force, what language or understanding can we adopt to understand these roles and how they play out? How could thinking about masculinity and femininity help us make sense of the dynamics that play out between us and our partner?

As well as being often confused with gender as described, this can be an extremely sensitive topic. It can be confused or overlaid with a sense that we 'should' be a certain way or that we must act in this or that manner to fit it. It has even been understood to have been created as an imperialist conspiracy to subjugate one group to the advantage of another[27]. While the focus here is not on the social and political rights and wrongs, no gender has a monopoly on "bad behaviour" as understood through the previous section on boundaries. We all can and do overstep boundaries at various times, in gross and subtle ways.

In terms of the dance, it is our business to invite our partner to dance or to choose to accept or decline such an invitation. Such an invitation and acceptance are very unlikely to breach any boundary, so long as they are made with respect. However, couples were clearly

---

[27] Gender by Meg-John Barker & Jules Scheele

choosing to dance together before any form of empire or colonialism came into play. A good starting point for this understanding - though not necessarily the origin - is to consider the Taoist notion of Yin and Yang.[28]

Understanding Yin and Yang

The Yin corresponds with the feminine and relates to our emotional aspects. It's the part of us that flows spontaneously towards the things that appeal to us, especially because of a positive feeling that we get from associating with those things. When we consider the things that inspire us such as a mountain or the ocean, we are contemplating the yin. It therefore expresses itself in poetry and music that conveys feeling, passion, and inspiration.

On the flipside, not all music is passionate and expressive. If you consider a military marching band, they may be creating music but it's of quite a different nature from music that is more spontaneous and expressive! This quality of structure, discipline and purpose is what is conveyed by the marching band, and this corresponds to the Yang. Rather than flowing with emotion, the Yang is 'on task' and working towards a goal, ideally in the shortest, most efficient way.

We may have preferences, but the marching band is ultimately neither better nor worse than any other kind of

---

[28] Tao De Ching by Laozi

music. However, it's very useful to be context aware because if one of the players in the marching band decides to shift into a spontaneous solo expressed from the heart, it may not be most welcome by the band leader!

With our dance analogy, the partner taking the role of leading the dance can be said to be in the Yang, and the one who is being led by the other plays the Yin role. Importantly, while one role is leading, it can't be said that one role is more important to making a beautiful dance. While either can dance alone, neither can capture the magic individually as a well-expressed dance between the two. It's in the interaction between the two that the dance is created, which can be seen as greater than the sum of the parts of either partner dancing alone.

The interplay of these dimensions in our relationships - whatever gender combination we may have - is a key factor in how the relationship goes. Just as in the dance, if we are misaligned in this respect, we can accurately predict the kinds of relationship challenges that we will experience.

Recognising our "Essence"

While we all can express aspects of both the Yin and Yang, for most people we find one of the roles more comfortable or natural than the other one. It is estimated that around 90% of people[29], <u>regardless of gender</u>, have a clear sense that being either the follower (Yin) or the leader (Yang) role in the dance feels more comfortable. If you picture yourself dancing with a partner, you may find it easy to sense which role feels better or you may need to practise to see which feels more comfortable.

Another way to consider is to think about the situations that feel the most comfortable and natural. So, if you thrive on having a goal, being on task and working towards that objective this might indicate that the yang or masculine is a more natural or intrinsic role. Whereas if you feel more comfortable when you are flowing, expressing your feelings or being creative this could indicate that you are more naturally towards the yin or feminine. Again, to reiterate, that there is nothing to say that being of male gender requires you to therefore have masculine essence or vice versa!

Other people can happily switch between roles and are equally happy whichever role we find ourselves playing. Again, there is no stigma here at all, we can choose to adopt any role that we choose or to switch as we wish, again regardless of gender.

However, what might happen if we find one or other role more natural but that we find ourselves acting in a way that doesn't fit with that role. Even outside of a relationship, let's say that we feel that we have a Yin

---

[29] The Way of the Superior Man, by David Deida

182

(feminine) essence, so that we like to follow, to flow and to express our emotionality. How would we get along if we placed ourselves in an environment where there was a high degree of discipline, structure, and rigidity? Let's say we joined the army and found ourselves in a life where we had limited opportunity to express our creativity and emotion. Even those qualities must be repressed or minimised to fulfil our duties. What chance of us being happy in an environment where we are unable to express these important and intrinsic aspects of who we are?

Being true to who we are

Coming back to the dancing analogy, let's imagine someone (in this example let's say a man called John) who feels much more comfortable in the role of leading his partner in a loving way through the dance. He is not only a competent dancer, but he loves dancing and he's looking forward to his evening of dancing in the salsa club. Everyone knows John, and he's a fun guy that everyone loves dancing with, and you can always rely on him for some good banter and fun.

On arrival, the teacher approaches him,

"Just to let you know John, the numbers are out so you're going to be a FOLLOWING partner this evening", the teacher tells him. "You're NOT going to lead tonight at all, and not just for one song either. For the whole evening!"

Is it possible that after a while - or very quickly - that John isn't having as much fun as he normally does. He's still dancing but he's just not flowing with this tonight.

"John, get over it," someone might say. "Have you got an ego problem or what, you seem to have a chip on your shoulder."

John is even misbehaving and making snarky comments, or he could have a look on his face making people think that he'd rather not be there. People are rotating partners, but NOBODY is enjoying the dancing when it comes to dancing with John. He's just not himself tonight.

Is there really something "wrong" with John, or has he adopted a role that just doesn't let him express himself in the way that he normally does? When he accepted the teacher's request to be the following partner, did he set himself up for an enjoyable night or has he gone along with an arrangement that isn't working for anyone? And it's not that he is not ABLE to perform the role of the follower - perhaps that even feels good occasionally and makes a nice change. But if there is a role that feels more natural (in this case the Yang / leader role) why would we want to take on the role that feels contrary to the one we enjoy the most?

When we both want to lead the dance

Continuing with the dancing analogy, what happens when both partners (of whatever gender combination) want to lead the dance at the same time.

"We're stepping back this way," one of them decides.

"Oh no we're not, we're doing a turn," the other commits.

Does this sound like a good formula for a beautiful dance? Are the partners of such a dance likely to be enjoying themselves? How long are they going to persist with this pattern?

If we take this analogy from the dance and into our relationship, what kind of communication challenges might such a couple be having?

"Why can we never agree?" they might wonder. "Today it's this issue and tomorrow it's another but it's like we're pulling in different directions and there is always a conflict."

When our styles of dancing don't fit

Another type of challenge could be when our dancing styles are misaligned. Let's say one of us wants to dance in a faster and more energetic way, and the other wants to flow in a more sensual and emotive way. We normally like to dance in the same style, and we've learned how our partner enjoys their dance and we've found a balance where everyone is comfortable.

But then one night, one of us really feels like expressing things differently in a different type of dance. If we are not able to communicate this clearly, is there any risk that the other may feel that their needs are not being met?

In this scenario, rather than coming together is a beautiful dance, the Yin and Yang don't manage to fuse their styles together but remain apart. It's always a choice to decide to dance with our partner, and at some times the gap may just feel too big to bridge. We're just not able to find a way of dancing that both enables us to express ourselves, while also enabling our partner to do the same.

Making sense of masculine and feminine communication styles

Whole books have been written about how masculine and feminine communication styles play out in relationships[30]. As we've seen, while this can often be oversimplified to say that this leads to challenges between men and women, this is only one of the many gender combinations in which we can experience this challenge. We can all move between distinctive styles of communication - from the feminine to the masculine and

---

[30] John Gray, Men are from Mars, Women are from Venus.

186

everywhere in between! It is context, essence, and relationship dependent.

Masculine communication: "It serves the purpose".

We looked at the masculine Yang quality earlier, so how does this show up in our communication style? From a masculine style we will tend to be more direct, and solution orientated. While we are being focussed on the problem at hand, there is at least a possibility that we may not be as emotionally connected or available as we might otherwise be! There are many problems in the world waiting to be solved though and this quality can be a wonderful thing. We will tend to be resourceful and focussed, as well as disciplined and resilient in working towards a meaningful solution.

Feminine communication: "It feels good".

At times that we are more driven by our Yin or feminine style we will tend to be more connected to our emotions and will therefore express those emotions more easily. We will be creative and spontaneous, while also being a good listener. We are likely to be receptive to understanding other people, and responsive to the emotions of others. The feelings we have could also be expressed by a high degree of care or nurturing for others as we pick up on the emotional state of the people around us. We are also likely to be more intuitive as we are sensitive to our own emotions and those of the people around us.

As discussed, we move between the distinctive styles during our life and during the day. The most appropriate style to adopt will depend on the needs of the moment.

For instance, if we are an army leader on a combat engagement and current information emerges about an immediate danger to the safety of our unit, it could be that urgent action needs to be taken. Once that decision is taken, it needs to be conveyed to others so that it can be acted on. This may be a time when direct and focussed communication is the most appropriate. If we were to spend those crucial seconds gauging the feelings of the team, it could come at a high cost.

If the cave person is fighting off the sabre-toothed tiger, it might not be the right time to engage him emotionally like asking for support or a hug!

"But hang on, there are no tigers," we might say. "We're in the twenty-first century here!"

But are there situations that could still *feel* like we have that level of focus and intensity that our ancestors might have felt when fending off wild animals? Let's say we work in a sales role, and we receive a new customer enquiry. The "tiger" could be that if we don't respond to the potential customer in a prompt way, they might purchase from a competitor. Or it could be that if we don't deliver a successful presentation at work, we may not progress in our job in the way we would like to. There may be no tiger, but that doesn't mean that we don't FEEL like there is a tiger!

In a different context though, say if we are relaxing and spending time with our partner, it could be useful to ensure that we are adequately engaging our emotions. Otherwise, there is a risk that they might not feel heard or supported. In this context, a more feminine communication style could be a useful quality to access.

"Ok I can see that this is really important to you and has been affecting you", we might say.

In this context it might be that no solution is being requested at all, but that what our partner wants is to feel heard and understood. If we jump into problem solving mode - at least too quickly - we might find ourselves picking up the pieces from an emotional disconnect or distancing.

Being consistent with our essence... most of the time!

The challenge here is that if we spend too much time in a style that doesn't fit with our essence, we can feel misaligned or even that we are losing ourselves! Let's take a person who is naturally and comfortably in the masculine style. It may be that his partner would love him to be more emotionally connected and sensitive, to enable a depth of empathy and feelings which could support the relationship. So far, so good up to a point. But what if this person spent all their time connecting with and expressing feelings, and therefore not in action mode. Could it be that such a person could start to feel frustrated and unable to express their natural gifts?

Similarly, if we naturally have a more emotive or feminine style (regardless as always of gender), how are we going to feel if the world around us including our partner is pushing us to be on task? It may be that an element of being on task is indeed useful, but if this need is too persistent and we are therefore not able to express our emotions effectively, how could this leave us feeling? Might we even get to a point of frustration where we don't even recognise ourselves anymore?

Flexing to support our partner.

One of the biggest challenges we need to overcome here is to find the balance between being true to ourselves while also being ready to flex to support our partner to meet their needs.

"I'm not looking for a solution here, I just need you to listen." they might say.

This may go against the grain of our tendency to be a problem solver - which again is a wonderful quality. But if we can't adapt ourselves to just be present to hear and acknowledge the feelings of our partner, we might find ourselves in a conflict or with emotional disconnection. At that point, no practical solution is going to help us.

Similarly, if our partner is "on task", we might need to defer our need to emotionally connect with them if we want to risk a different type of disconnection.

"I've got a really important deadline, and I'd be grateful if you could only disturb me if there is really an emergency for the next two hours," they might say.

After a few minutes we might feel compelled to share an exciting update that one of our friends has just got into a new relationship. But what kind of reaction might we get if we disturb the partner who is "on task", to share our excitement about this news? It could be that sharing this development has to just wait for a time when our partner is able to be more receptive to it. Otherwise, we might find ourselves hurt that they are not as excited as we are, because they are focussed on completing or achieving something!

Heart-felt Dialogue

Is there a way to work directly on our communication habits to give ourselves the best possible chance of having a positive outcome? Imagine having a structure to work through that means that we are really heard by our partner, and that we want to come together to find resolutions that really work for both of us. This is something that we work through with our clients in detail, and which is often described as one of the most impactful areas of improvement in the overall relationship[31].

This process can be used for any important topic of conversation, though in general it's only going to be necessary where there is an emotional component to the conversation. That means that we are going to be worried or concerned about something, or that we feel that it's important to let our partner know how we feel about it. If it's simple information that we are conveying like our favourite television programme is about to start and to find out whether they would like to join us, it's not generally going to be required!

Examples of good times to use it would include:
- Sharing our concern about an upcoming commitment or engagement
- Letting our partner know how proud we were of how they dealt with a recent situation.
- Raising an issue from a recent interaction that wasn't resolved in a positive way.
- Celebrating a recent personal or joint success that was particularly meaningful.
- Letting our partner know about some bad feeling or resentment that has arisen from a previous conversation.
- Processing or thinking about the lessons learnt from an event that didn't go according to plan.

---

[31] Developed from work by Harville Hendrix sometimes referred to as Imago dialogue.

Note that these examples are not necessarily problems or 'complaints' but can also be the opportunity to express positive successes!

Check your emotional state BEFORE you open your mouth!

Are there times when things get on top of us, and we're not able to manage our emotions in the way that we are dealing with a situation. Using our analogy from earlier we could say at these times that despite our best efforts to stay "on the bridge", we nevertheless find ourselves in the river of our emotions fighting for air. It's therefore important to have the self-awareness to know that there are simply moments when that important conversation might need to wait! Even though it feels like it's just got to happen right now, if we do proceed then it may not give us the best chance of reaching a positive conclusion.

One of the foundations of the work we do with individuals and couples is giving us ways to enhance and develop our emotional state, so that we have this self-awareness.

We are always looking for an understanding that gets us BEYOND our coping mechanisms, rather than just looking for a way to refine and hone them. And it's also true that at these times we need to see whether the coping mechanisms we are deploying are functional or whether they are causing additional issues. For instance, taking some fresh air as a coping mechanism could be less damaging than turning to alcohol!

In any case, the point here is that we need to learn to be honest and self-reflective enough to recognise that we are being triggered and that it might be more helpful to deal with ourselves and then to come back to our partner to raise that concern.

Agree a time to talk - DON'T assume!

In relationships - and especially in long-term relationships - we can get lazy in our thinking. Do we ever for instance feel that because they are our partner, the other person should be available to drop whatever they are doing right now and be available to talk to us? That no matter how critical the task that they are doing, or whatever commitments they might have to other people - a boss or a client, for example - that they will put that aside at a moment's notice.

"No, you don't get it," you might think. "This is a real emergency!"

It's worth at least considering whether the issue at hand is a genuine emergency that couldn't wait at least a few hours, if necessary, before being dealt with. Aside from critical medical situations, most of the challenges that we need to raise with our partner will not be exacerbated by the patience to plan our conversation in

194

advance. And it might be that our partner is available right now - but that is different from ASSUMING or thinking that they SHOULD be available right now!

If we start the conversation in this considered and respectful way, does that make the other person more or less likely to be similarly respectful towards ourselves? And does it give us a better or worse chance of reaching a positive resolution and connection through the conversation?

Also, if we are the person being asked for an appointment, it's worth considering the best way to respond. For instance, if now really isn't a convenient time could we at least PROPOSE an alternative. If we don't and it's as simple as, "you're not on the list and you're not coming in", what could that convey?

In addition, it would be helpful if the time that we propose isn't too far into the future. There is no set guideline, but in general if the proposed time is more than a few hours into the future, and certainly more than forty-eight hours it could convey a lack of interest or priority on our side.

"Sure, we can talk, come back in 3 weeks and I'll fit you in," might not show the level of care and interest that our partner is looking for!

Set your intention BEFORE jumping in!

If you've ever had an interaction where you didn't reach a positive or satisfactory conclusion, it's worth considering how clearly, we framed the conversation at the outset.

"Hang on, you're giving me a solution here, when all I wanted was for you to listen and to hear me out," we might complain.

But did we make that intention clear from the outset, or did we simply assume that our partner is a mind reader and should know that this was our goal? If they misunderstand our intention, whose fault is that really if we haven't been explicit from the outset?

In addition, being explicit about our intention helps us both get clear and to hold ourselves accountable that we are still on track.

"A few minutes ago, I'd understood that this conversation was about finding a solution to this problem, but now I'm getting the feeling that it's more about point scoring from this other challenge we experienced."

Share your issue.

The point above about managing our emotions is also important to remember as we start to share the issue that's on our mind. We need to keep some level of

196

objectivity, while also honouring and recognising that we might have strong feelings that need to be expressed. In addition, we need to avoid overwhelming our partner from the outset and giving them time to process and digest what we are saying. They have agreed to hear us out, but let's also give them a chance to reflect as we share.

The sharing will be a balance between the facts as we see them, and our feelings relating to those facts. The exact balance will depend on context but remember if there is no feeling at all then this process may not be necessary.

Reflect back to ensure understanding.

This is where the person listening or 'receiving' the issue needs to practise what is sometimes called 'active listening'. We need to be focussed and attentive and to give the person a feeling that we are present and interested in what they are raising. This isn't the time to be watching television or checking your phone, remembering that we've agreed that now is the time to talk.

"Ok so what I'm hearing is…", would be a typical way to periodically reflect back our understanding.

During this reflecting back we are mindful of not changing the subject or getting defensive which is often what happens when conversation breaks down. A good analogy for this process is that we are trying to get ourselves out of the way to be like a mirror. In this sense we are not colouring the situation but simply reflecting back what we hear in a neutral way.

Draw out further points.

Often when we start sharing around an issue, we can find that it's multi-layered. This means that the first statement that we make about an issue is not the core point that we need to express. For example, we might start sharing concerns about an upcoming holiday before getting to the real point that it's the way a certain family dynamic plays out when we're on holiday that is our real concern. If we don't uncover the nugget of truth here, the danger is that we come up with a solution - to the WRONG problem and end up unsatisfied or going around in circles!

"Is there anything else you want to tell me about that...?", is a great question to deploy here.

This gives our partner the gift of a safe space to keep going until they reach completion and that the issues have been put on the table. While it requires a degree of discipline to follow, we can often see our partner visibly relax and open up as we give them that opportunity to really let us know what is on their mind. There is no set number of times that we need to ask this question as our partner reveals the issue on their mind.

"Wait a minute," you might think. "My partner can talk and talk so this is going to take forever."

On the flipside, how long does it take when you are going around in cycles of frustration because someone is feeling unheard and that we are missing the point? Also, if we consider that part of the purpose is to enhance connection, isn't this time well spent?

Your partner has a valid point!

The term 'gaslighting' has come to be understood as behaviour which comes to make someone doubt their reality. It originates from a play[32] where a character manipulates the level of the lighting in the home to convince another that she is mentally unwell for the purpose of manipulation. It's used to refer to that sinking feeling of "am I going mad here", when despite our best efforts we are simply unable to make ourselves understood and we FEEL that the person is being deliberately difficult. However, it can be done in a way that makes the feeling difficult to validate or substantiate leading us to feel unstable or anxious.

A critical point is that the fact of my partner simply having a different point of view and being unwilling to give it up to concede to our own point of view, is NOT gaslighting! We are each entitled to a point of view - that's each of our business!

---

[32] Gas Light by Patrick Hamilton, 1938

Beyond that context, the point here is that we want to do the OPPOSITE of gaslighting by validating the logic of what the person says. Imagine the feeling of reassurance that we gain by the fact that someone else acknowledges that what we are saying makes sense - at least from our own perspective!

The key objection at this point is that we don't agree with the other person, so why would we want to validate them?

"If I validate them, that means that I'm going along and agreeing with what they say," we think.

By validating the other person does not mean that we ourselves agree or otherwise. In fact, to agree OR disagree at this point would be a breakdown in the process, as we are still playing the role of the mirror in reflecting back what we have heard. If we colour what we hear or give our own perspective this is subtly but importantly making it about us rather than them.

We are looking for some simple logic that confirms that what they are saying has some logic or reason about it.

"Well, it makes sense that if you feel uncomfortable when my mother is here, and she's visiting next week that you'd want to raise this with me now."

Versus:

"Yes, I see what you mean, and agree that she can be awkward," is INCORRECT as it's stating YOUR opinion which is turning the point around to yourself which is premature. You are going to give your perspective but later in the process!

"How dare you criticise my mum when yours is so much worse", would be even further off-track, as this takes over the conversation completely. If we are not willing to hear our partner out, how likely are they to do the same when it's our turn? If we simply change the subject as a form of defensiveness and distraction, what chance do we have of making our partner feel heard and coming to a resolution of the challenge at hand.

Recognise their feelings!

When we are struggling in our relationship, empathy can seem in short supply. On the other hand, if we value emotional closeness in our relationship, it's critical that we learn to accept and acknowledge each other's feelings. As we pointed out earlier, this process is going to be used for situations where there is some emotional component - otherwise we wouldn't be using it.

"Well, I can see that this is important to you, and causing you some stress", works for instance. We are listening out for an expression of concern, anxiety, anger, or some other feeling that is affecting the other person. Once we hear that we simply put that into words which may be the same as the ones they used, or our understanding of the feelings that they expressed.

"I'd feel the same if I were in your situation," is INCORRECT as this is again turning things around to ourselves and how we anticipate that we'd deal with a given situation. We'd feel the same, or maybe we wouldn't but it's very easy to lose the magic in this process once we make it about how we ourselves would relate to this challenge.

Again, to recognise the other person's feelings does NOT require us to feel the same or to agree with their assessment of what is happening. Even if we think the person is being ridiculous and over-reacting, it's essential that we contain any such judgement and ensure that the other person feels that their emotions are valid and acceptable. Remember that you will have the chance to give your side of things later in the process!

Ensure space for both partners.

Once we've been given the space to really be heard, would it be reasonable to give the same gift to our partner? They are also entitled to a point of view about the matter which is going to build mutual understanding and lead us in the direction of a solution that works for both of us. What could you say about a person who is happy to give their opinion and demand to be heard out, but is not happy to do the same for their partner?

We are looking to repeat the same steps above but changing the role so that the person sharing now becomes the person listening, validating, and empathising. Once completed, the process can continue again with the roles switching back, until both partners feel that they have expressed what they need to share about the subject at hand or related matters.

Develop options.

Sometimes just through the act of respectfully hearing each other out and giving each other that space, there may be no action required at all! The issue may be just that we need to express our feelings about something that simply needs to be lived with. It's about financial stress that we are feeling, or an issue about how we feel overwhelmed by the needs of a sick relative. We already know what we need to do, and we have it in hand, but we feel a lot better having been listened to.

In other cases, there will be actions that are required to address the issue that has been brought forward. We will usually move into options naturally from a point of being heard by our partner. In addition, having done the previous steps we are likely to be more open to finding agreement and compromise that we would otherwise have been!

If our partner puts forward an idea, it's useful at this point to repeat it to ensure a common understanding before we jump into any conversation of evaluating whether it can work. We may then want to develop or revise the idea in some way, or we may simply say that this is a useful idea.

In any case, we are looking to develop several different ideas at this point rather than one. If we are putting all our hope on one solution it can be like having all our eggs in one basket! In addition, it can be extremely useful to have timeframes around the actions so that we can consider agreeing to a course of action "for the next 4 weeks", rather than looking to agree something indefinitely or leaving it vague and open-ended.

Select one, for now!

Having got to this point and built a high level of respect through the process it's essential that we remember that any action is only agreed if it is acceptable to BOTH parties. It's also useful to plan to review the progress at a certain point in time, and to even put that in the calendar. This means that we are agreeing to run with a solution for now while accepting that we are going to evaluate in the future to see how things are working out. We might need to tweak it in the future depending on how things go.

Recognise your partner.

There are many reasons why expressing thanks at the end of the conversation is a wonderful way to wrap things up! Firstly, the issue that your partner has raised was something that we were not aware of to the same extent as we are now, so our partner has supported us to a deeper understanding of the point in hand. Also, that our partner didn't have to give up their time for this conversation, but they have CHOSEN to do so to support us. In addition, if we've followed the steps successfully, we are both likely to be feeling less concerned and better understood and therefore in a better frame of mind. And if we say thank you, they are more likely to want to engage in this process in the future - that they are valued. The list goes on!

Easier said than done!

If this approach sounds appealing, you might find that the in-depth work we do around this with our clients may be of benefit for your relationship. While a straightforward process, this does not mean that it's easy to implement in practice without some important foundations being in place. The benefits once we do really master this approach pay off over a whole lifetime.

If you want to gauge whether you might benefit from this work, complete the Scorecard on the homepage of our website to get some instant tailored feedback on your own relationship.

Breakthrough 3 - Love is expressed in my relationship.

If we are looking to create or transform a loving relationship, it's worth considering what is going to make the relationship an expression of love, rather than anything else. Do we even deliberately decide what love looks like to us, and whether that understanding is the same as or even like that of our partner?

Love - a learned concept!

While a young baby may be able to experience a feeling or sensation of love - for example when playing with a parent or caregiver - we must learn the meaning of love. If the baby sees one person in the room acting in a way that we might describe as loving, and someone else behaving in another way (let's say angry), the baby will have no vocabulary to be able to categorise or describe those behaviours. We can say that a grouping of behaviours that we can label in such a way is an 'emotion concept'[33], while each example of such a behaviour is an 'instance' of that behaviour. As we develop our vocabulary, we learn different concepts which may become more nuanced as we learn, read and experience life. As a toddler we may see behaviour as 'angry', but later as we develop, we make a finer distinction between 'jealous' and 'enraged', for example.

---

[33] Lisa Feldman Barrett, How Emotions are Made.

One of the joys of learning a language is finding words that are an equivalent of something that we understand, as well as words for which there is no direct translation. Take *Age-otori* in Japanese for instance. This is the moment of realisation on leaving the barbers or hairdresser and realising that our hair looks worse than it did before we went in. It's a unique combination of shame, pain and having thrown away our money in futility that we can't go back and easily remedy! As we don't have this word in English, it's very difficult to convey the feeling without describing it with a few related words.

The point here is that our understanding of the emotion concept of 'love' is not an absolute or unique phenomenon but something that we have learned from our environment and the world around us. So even if we've grown up in a similar culture to our partner, could it be that the understanding of love that we've developed is different in important ways. When we have a cultural difference, this can be taken to another level altogether.

Let's say that one person's understanding of love is that when I have a problem, we share it together and work together to resolve it. But their partner's understanding of love is that if I have a problem I resolve it under the radar, so that my partner doesn't need to worry about me and that it doesn't affect them or our relationship. Can we say that one is incorrect? No, they are simply different understandings that we have come to.

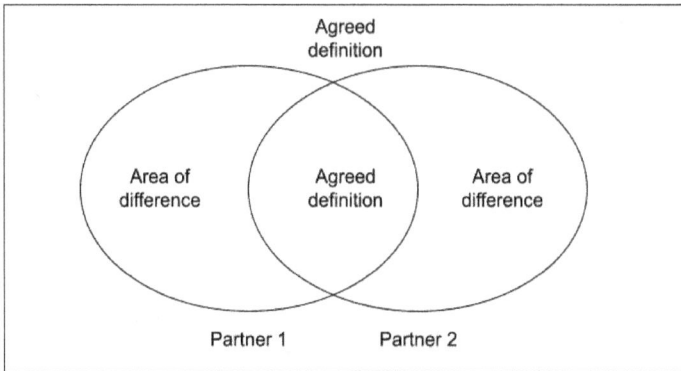

In the diagram, you can see that there is an intersection where both partners would agree that certain acts or behaviours would come under a definition of love. Let's say we both agree that greeting each other warmly when we are reunited would be an instance of love. We see it the same way.

But then there are areas when one or the other partner would understand something to be love, whereas the other person would not. For example, one may say that when it's someone's birthday we would drop everything on that day to spend the whole day with that person and that would be considered love. The other partner though would not include this necessarily in their definition. Unless the other person has expressly asked for this to be arranged, they would personally prefer to work and not make a big deal about their birthday.

And then there are things which are outside of both circles where they would both immediately agree that a behaviour would not come under a definition of love. They both agree that not going to bed at the same time as their partner would not fall under a definition of love.

Raising our standards - living in love

It is sometimes said that we don't necessarily get our goals, but we always get our standards[34]. So, what could be the standards that we set or understand regarding the kind of interactions, experiences, and emotions that we'd like to experience with our partner, and how can we move more towards those kinds of experiences?

Fear versus love

In our work with couples and individuals we explore the various kinds of emotion that we tend to experience and look at how we can move towards the ones that we want. It's worth considering how often variants of fear can be the ones that hold us back from moving towards a loving experience in our relationship and in life in general. Sometimes those feelings are linked to fear such as anxiety, apprehension, and worry. At other moments the feeling of other negative emotions like anger, jealousy or resentment may have fear lurking under the surface. Maybe it's fear of being wrong, of

---

[34] As quoted by Tony Robbins

abandonment or of conflict that gets expressed by these other emotions.

The way that we can immediately know that we're living more towards fear is that we have a sense of being stuck in a negative cycle. It's like we can't win and that everything we do to resolve the problem just seems to bring us back to the same frustration. Maybe it's a reactive tit-for-tat or maybe we just don't address the problems but brush them under the carpet. Either way, we go around in circles and not much seems to change.

At the other end of the scale, we have the more positive emotions of trust, acceptance, gratitude, and joy that tend to work as an antidote to these more negative emotions. It's worth considering where we tend to reside on that scale and the quality of life and relationships that are likely to go hand in hand with such emotions. The good news is that it's very much something that we can work on if we so choose. Just like the physically unfit person can be confident of improvement if they implement consistently, the emotionally unfit person can also be assured of positive results once we do this work. It's not a question of whether it works, but rather a question of whether we want to do the work!

Doing the work!

We tend to know the kinds of habits, behaviours and attitudes that move us towards love versus the ones that have kept us stuck in the cycle of fear. The thing that we don't have is consistency and this is where our programme gives us the resources AND accountability to really follow through rather than just picking up some glib advice or tips from a magazine article or a social media meme!

Choosing our partner

Have you ever been in a relationship with a feeling that your partner is not choosing you? They are trying to support us in some ways that are meaningful to THEM, but they are not doing the thing that would be meaningful to us, and to make us feel really chosen. It's much more than just 'knowing our partner's love language', though this is a useful starting point.

Are we speaking the same language?

One of the most widely quoted concepts around relationships is the idea that there are different languages for how we express love[35]. If we are not speaking the same language, it's argued that we may not connect, and experience love together despite our best intentions:

1. Giving gifts is the expression of love through physical or non-physical objects.
2. Quality time is when we show our affection through the spending of time with our partner.

---

[35] Gary Chapman, The Five Love Languages

3. Acts of service is demonstrating love through practical and other support.
4. Words of affirmation is encouragement and support of our partner through words or writing.
5. Physical touch is the expression of love through touch.

Through the book, the languages are developed and each also breaks down into dialects or sub-languages to help us get more clarity on what is most important for us. The key takeaway is that the language that we ourselves prefer to experience love, is not necessarily the same one as our partner. This can lead to disconnection and misunderstanding.

Beyond love languages

As well as understanding what my partner's love language is, the key question is really whether we do those actions that enable each other to feel loved. I might understand that quality time is important to my partner, but do I make that a priority? If I do those things, I can say that in those moments I am choosing my partner rather than choosing something else, for example my work or myself. We may understand that something is important - let's say to keep fit - but it is another thing to do the actions consistently that will enable us to build those qualities.

Another useful way of thinking about whether we are conveying love is to consider what we understand by the idea of benevolence[36]. The opposite of benevolence is "malevolence":

"The quality of causing or wanting to cause harm or evil."[37]

Have you ever experienced a close relationship where this quality was at play, even some of the time? If so - or even if you can only imagine such a relationship - does this feel like love in any way? If wanting to cause harm or evil to another person does not seem like an expression of love, what is the opposite? In what ways could we express benevolence towards our partner in our relationship?

Breakthrough 4 - Any inter-dependency is healthy and functional.

Our lives are intertwined.

Whether we've been in previous relationships before or not, we always bring our own legacy into the

---

[36] Russell Brand, Revelation

[37]

https://dictionary.cambridge.org/dictionary/english/malevolence

relationship. The things we bring may be tangible like children or financial assets, or we bring emotional resources and experience that we are ready to put into our relationship. In any case, as soon as our worlds meet each other, it's inevitable that these aspects that we bring are going to be affected by each other.

It's like if we arrive together at a clearing in the forest and decide that this is going to be the spot where we are going to construct our home[38]. We each bring resources and ideas and decide that this new entity is going to come into life in this place through our joint work and inspiration. The decisions that we make about the form and construction of that house are going to affect ourselves and potentially others around us that live in or visit that house in future.

At this point that we decide to enter a relationship together we begin to build, and we can see that our lives begin to link together, as if they are intertwined. We depend on our partner, and we are affected by the decisions each of us makes. In fact, in many cases it will be necessary to consult each other because of the inevitability of how a decision taken by one will impact the other. Some of those impacts we may see immediately, while others may be less clear in the moment, with the impacts developing over time.

---

[38] Shared by Matthew Hussey

If we are not willing or able to be mindful and respectful of how our decisions affect others, is it even viable to try to build something together? We'd consider just building something on our own instead.

Our commitment to the relationship

To take another analogy, is it possible for a tree to grow to maturity without having its roots deep in the ground? Not only can the tree not take the nutrients and moisture from the soil without a root structure, but how would it cope when the winds of life start to blow?

If we want our relationship to resemble a great tree in any way, it's worth considering what it means to have roots in the ground. Imagine for instance that we are ready to walk away at the first challenge or growing pain, is it ever going to be possible for a powerful awe-inspiring tree to ever grow. If we have any hope of resting one day in the shade of such a tree, are we therefore open to participating in the creation and nurturing of such a tree, and staying the course?

Or the tree that we want to grow is something that we ourselves want full control of, and the idea of jointly cultivating a tree with a loving partner just isn't part of our blueprint.

Giving up sovereignty for the greater good

The analogy of a trade agreement is a useful perspective to considering our relationship commitments. When countries or regions enter into trade agreements they commit to certain terms or restrictions. For instance, a country might commit to accepting goods or services from another without the tariffs or controls that would otherwise apply. In a sense, it is giving up some autonomy or control that it has the right to exert because of some agreed mutual benefit. This is a conscious decision to give-up - at least temporarily - some sovereignty in exchange for another benefit, which might be the same or equivalent in exchange, at least for an agreed time.

When we enter a relationship, we can also see it as a giving up of a level of sovereignty. For instance, many people in committed relationships give up the choice to have intimate relationships with other people that they could otherwise have if they were not in that relationship. Again, it's a conscious choice to give up something because we are receiving benefits in other ways. It could be reciprocal or there may be another benefit that we are looking to receive.

Choosing our relationship every day

As with the trade agreement, we may re-evaluate the deal at some point and decide that what we are giving up is no longer compensated by the benefits that we are receiving. This again brings us to a tension that we are always managing through our relationship. While we can only create something meaningful with commitment, we always have the choice to make a different decision if we feel that it is no longer viable for any reason.

The key is to remember that we are each making a choice, and that we or our partner retain the freedom to make different choices if we wish. In this sense we can honour our partner and to value and cherish every day that we continue to make that choice to stay together. The alternative is a lazy feeling that they are simply doing what they have promised to do, and that the only choice available to them is to hold out until the end.

How does that sound as a recipe for creating a magic relationship?

Honouring our separateness

Having our own individual heritage and experience, we are each bringing valuable resources to the relationship. While we are committing energy and resources to building something together, this does not mean that we cease to have our own individual expressions and projects. It would be difficult to throw EVERYTHING we have into this joint project, without eventually having a sense that we have lost something of ourselves. It may be that in the context of our joint project, space is respected for personal expression so that we can keep in touch with our own passions.

A common challenge in relationships is that we can be consumed by the relationship and try to make it work, and we then lose touch with other aspects of our life that are important to us. We had a strong friendship group, but that we just do not make the time any more to maintain those connections.

"That's ok though," we might think. "My family needs me, and they come first."

It's worth considering what needs to happen though to enable us to sustainably show up in the right way for our family, and that it may require some time or energy to be devoted to other activities.

The relationship gives us freedom.

A more empowering perspective is to consider how the relationship gives us freedom. Are there ways that we can create new possibilities through our relationship that we wouldn't otherwise have. My new partner can engage with my children in a way that gives them an experience that they otherwise would not have. This sense of freedom can add to a healthy interdependence rather than the flavour of feeling trapped and without choices that can come with co-dependency.

Living in adult-adult mode

Transactional Analysis is a therapeutic model developed in the 1950s[39] which explores how different "ego states" relate to one another. The components are parent,

---

[39] https://en.wikipedia.org/wiki/Transactional_analysis

adult, and child. The qualities of "parenting" include support, encouragement, nurturing, and the metaphoric arm around the shoulder. One idea that we might carry is that as we mature and become more independent and adult-like should we *completely* lose the need to be parented. While we might reduce our dependence on these, is it reasonable to expect that as feeling beings we would ever completely remove these needs?

It's a useful perspective to consider in intimate relationships, especially to understand the impact of parent to child dynamics that might emerge and how they affect our intimate relationship. If we ever have a sense that our partner is parenting us, or that we ourselves take on the role of the parent how does this sit alongside other aspects of the relationship.

For instance, if our partner is playing the role of a child in one moment, then making a sexual advance the next these may not sit comfortably together! At the times when we have needs of reassurance and support, would it be better to meet those through our partner or through others - such as our biological parents or friends?

As with many aspects of this work there is no ultimate right or wrong although there can be mismatches in expectations. One partner might be comfortable sitting in the parent or child role for fifty percent of the time whereas the other might only be willing to entertain that dynamic for only ten percent of the time for instance.

This is an area that we explore further through our work, and it's one area where a form of therapy can be useful.

"It's weird, my partner is really loving but I get a feeling that a child is there with me in the room, and I don't get it," we might think. Often there may be an unprocessed experience or trauma from childhood that the person has been unable or unwilling to move beyond and remains trapped in the past. They may need professional support to deal with any challenging emotions that were created at that point so that they can fully move on.

Being capable of autonomy and independence

One of the ways that we can ensure that we stay primarily in adult roles is to maintain a sense that even when we have chosen to act as a unit or team, we are at least capable of acting alone if we choose to do so. Even when we may not choose to exercise that decision to function independently, we are clear that we would still be able to function and live our life in the case that our partner was not willing or able to support us in any or all areas.

"If you were to leave, I'd just fall apart completely," we might say. While this might give us a sense of bonding, closeness, or reassurance that our partner would never leave us, how does this sense of dependence impact on the relationship? Is that the kind of bonding we really want, and is that a fair and healthy level of responsibility to impose upon our partner?

Sharing power fairly and openly

Another related area to explore is whether power is shared in a way that sits comfortably for both partners. We may have a sense that our partner has too much control over us, either financially or in terms of making us do things that we don't want to do or preventing us from doing things that we want to do. Or it may be that we've settled into a role where it is us that seems to take more responsibility for the other person that we feel comfortable with. Again, this would imply that an unhealthy power dynamic has developed and while there may not be an ultimate right and wrong, there are certainly situations that feel uncomfortable. We may have a sense that we have lost control of the trajectory of our life and that we are not able to follow goals that are meaningful to us. This is highly likely to lead to a level of resentment and may be unsustainable in the long term.

In addition, as we mature it could be that our tolerance for such situations reduces. For instance, it may have suited us to be looked after while we felt powerless but that we look to re-establish our independence as we grow in confidence or other resources.

If our wellbeing or emotions are the responsibility of someone else, are we still empowered to be in control of our life?

"I feel bad, and it's your fault," we might think or say.

While we are certainly impacted by the behaviour of others, how do we feel when we make our feelings the responsibility of others? Even when we might feel that we've been a victim of someone's actions, is it true that we have lost control over the course of events? For instance, are we really forced to be around that person who is impacting us negatively. Other than being imprisoned and forced to share a cell with that person, we have the freedom to decide who we surround ourselves with.

Breakthrough 5 - My relationship is dynamic and fun

While our relationships might be the context in which we live our domestic lives, what happens when all we have left is our domestic arrangements. If the only thing we can see is an endless cycle of taking the kids to school, going to work, and making dinner it can suck the energy and passion out of life and of our relationship. And it's not that those things are not important either. Maybe we love the school run, and seeing our children dealing with their homework and progressing but how could it affect

our relationship if this is the only focus of our daily
activities?

If we feel that this need is not being met, and that we
don't see a healthy path to meeting it, could we find
ourselves looking for excitement and fun in ways that
could be detrimental or unhealthy?

The Three Stages of Relationships

How can we think about the various stages that we go
through in our relationship, and how to identify and
navigate the key challenges of each? It's helpful to
break the relationship down into three stages that occur
broadly in sequence[40].

Stage 1 - Romantic Love

When we first get together with a partner it can be an
intense experience! In fact, even the sense of
anticipation that there is this person to whom we feel
drawn and who is open to pursuing a connection with us
can set our hearts racing! The energy and buzz that
propels us at this moment is the fuel of countless
stories, songs and films that provide a constant draw to
audiences around the world.

When we experience this, it can be overwhelming, as
every waking thought is taken up by thinking of this
person. Every (even slight!) quality that we appreciate is

---

[40] Harville Hendrix - Finding and Keeping Love

magnified, and every potential flaw is minimised or put to one side.

"Aww, he even plays the guitar... can you imagine," we might tell our friends in blissful awe.

"I mean, he does have a bit of a temper on him... but it's not ALL the time, mostly he's really cute," we might say.

Missing the 'red flags'

Importantly, we often do see the warning signs at this stage. We register that there is something that could well develop into a problem over time. It's that they don't share an important value that we hold such as respect towards animals, or that they tend to withdraw or sulk when we can't agree on something.

The issue isn't that we aren't aware of those challenges, it's just that we decide - consciously or unconsciously - to put them to one side for now as we enjoy the ride! It's like we're enjoying the buzz so much that we don't want to allow any inconvenient factors to spoil the fun!

Drug fuelled hedonism.

Even in the absence of any drugs that we might choose to use, there are no shortage of highs and lows during this phase. Our bodies are a potent cocktail with the function of dopamine often playing a substantial role in the rollercoaster that we are on. In the same way that the gambling addict feels physically drawn to the betting shop, we have a similar intense need to see our partner. This can be felt extremely intensely, and we are similarly rewarded with a rush of pleasure when we finally get our fix!

This stage is characterised by high highs and low lows, and it is this factor that can lead us to become addicted. It's like our day-to-day life struggles to give us this level of intensity, and just like the drug addict the subsequent low can be a challenging period to endure. So, we look again for the high, and the cycle continues.

Stage 2 - The Power Struggle

There comes a stage though when we are no longer able to ignore the issues that have been so far put to one side. Maybe we're having a bad day, or maybe the issue occurs at a time that makes it more of an issue than it was in the past. Let's say the issue is that our partner leaves the kitchen in a mess in the morning.

"Oh, what a lovely mess," we normally think, as we skip around the kitchen clearing up after them.

But today we're running late for work, and we've got friends coming over later where we want to make the right impression and then we reach a threshold. Now the truth of what we have been already observing becomes irrefutable and we know that this cannot go on anymore, so we have a showdown. Possibly immediately or otherwise we contain ourselves until the right moment, but either way we know that this has gone on long enough.

When we do eventually raise the issue, there is at least a possibility that our partner may also have a gripe or two that they themselves have been holding back. Now the gloves are off and everything is open for discussion. It's like if they are going to raise this bad habit of ours, they must be ready to address one or two of their own!

Calling it a day

At this point, some people will think that because the relationship isn't quite as magical as we first thought then we are obviously not 'soul mates', or 'twin flames', or whatever terms we choose. It seems to us that our partner is not worthy of the pedestal that we have been placing them on, and since they are not perfect then the relationship is just not meant to be.

"I'm bored of this conversation already," we think. Now we're feeling the heat of criticism rather than the heat of passion and we start to consider whether this relationship business is all fun and light after all.

At this stage, some people will simply leave the relationship. They might feel let down that the unrealistically high expectations that they had set for their partner have not been met, so they may even leave with some resentment. This sense of being ready to leave at the first problem is sometimes referred to as the 'avoidant' attachment style meaning that they deal with the difficulty by avoiding the other person, in this case by walking out.

"Well, we're not getting along very well..." they think. "But on the other hand, I've got twenty messages on this dating app from people who seem really fun and are not going to give me this grief over the mess in the kitchen!" or whatever the challenge is. Maybe I can even rekindle the flame with one of those people I was messaging before.

The avoidant person then leaves and re-joins the ranks of the dating pool and gets recycled through the process. This is why the dating pool often seems like it's full of avoidant people that struggle with commitment or overcoming these kinds of challenges.

Working through to the other side

Other couples do manage to successfully navigate the Power Struggle by finding a deeper understanding, through effective communication and finding compromises that work for both parties. It's important to honour our own needs while also having the flexibility to adapt to the challenges that our partner expresses.

Sometimes everything comes up together and we can reconcile everything through a single cycle of the process. At other times it can be multi-layered where we work through several challenges, but then additional factors come up at a later point which need to be discussed and resolved.

Many of our clients come to us during this phase, when they are struggling to work through the issues that have come to the surface.

Stage 3 - Enduring Love

If we manage to navigate the Power Struggle, we can enter the third stage where the love and connection we feel has a vastly different flavour. Rather than being dopamine fuelled highs and lows during Romantic Love, we can experience a deeper connection as well as forming a stable unit where we can work together towards a common goal.

If our only relationship experiences up to this point have been in Romantic Love, this can be a confusing adaptation to make. We might even think that there is something missing, or that it's just boring. This is where we need to consider what our vision is for our life, as ultimately, we may not be ready or willing to settle into this stage of deeper connection. We may still be hooked to the thrill of the rollercoaster, or we just decide that our days on the rollercoaster haven't yet run their course!

"Hang on, I want to be out partying and having fun, and all I seem to do is change smelly nappies," we might think.

On the flipside, for as long as our focus is on riding roller coasters it may be difficult to create a lasting connection that stands the test of time and enables us to experience long term connection with a partner.

While it's only during Enduring Love that we can build a life together of commitment and connection, there is inevitably the in-built challenge that things can feel at times far less magical than during Romantic Love. So how do we counteract the issues of domesticity and boredom which could otherwise be passion killers and lead us to look for that excitement elsewhere?

It's worth considering the kinds of activities that we did at the start of the relationship and thinking about how we could maintain those in some way. Could the things that we did that led us to feeling that level of connection give us any clues as to what we could do now to re-build or maintain them? We checked in during our working day with our partner to see how they were doing, or we thought of sharing small gifts to express our appreciation of them.

It's also worth assessing our rituals and practices and seeing how they support our relationship. For example, did we previously eat our evening meal together, whereas now we've moved to eating mainly separately? Or did we previously go to bed at the same time whereas now one person tends to go to sleep earlier meaning that we lose a moment of connection before we go to sleep. Whichever rituals are important to us through the day, they give us hints at the ways that we are prioritising our relationship or choosing our partner.

Walking together on the same path

Many companies - especially larger ones - develop and publish a vision or mission statement showing what the company stands for. For anyone lower down the hierarchy who has been presented with this lofty form of words by senior management we may not have a particularly positive view of this exercise! However, the exercise can be powerful and clarifying in bringing any differences to the surface and having a sense of being on the same page.

Very few couples or families possess such a statement of intent of what we stand for and where we are heading that can work as a unifying force[41]. We know from the work we do with couples that this can be an enormously powerful exercise, and one that many have involved their children in. Even young children tend to love the sense of working together, and that other people are interested about what matters to them. Naturally they will engage on their level and express the kinds of interests and priorities that matter to them. One couple shared how the thing that was important to their young daughter was that when it rained, she could go out in her wellies to jump in the puddles!

---

[41] Stephen Covey, The 7 Habits of Highly Successful Families

Once this process is completed you have a statement or image that represents everyone's goals that can help you stay on track during good and challenging times alike. It can enable you to celebrate achievements and behaviour that is consistent with the statement as well as to question other behaviour which may not.

Deepening our connection every day

It is possible to spend a lot of time with somebody without really strengthening our connection, or to spend a brief time and to feel much closer. We might be sitting on the sofa side by side with each person on their phone for instance doing their own thing. Sure, we're together physically but how much closer emotionally do we feel at the end of it? Also, there is a balance here and sometimes it might well feel good to do our own things such as reading different books.

If we value that sense of connection, it's important to find activities and exercises that enable us to get to know each other on a deeper level.

"We're together all the time so of course we know each other," we might think. Though it's incredible the improvements that clients report once we take a more structured approach to ensuring that we are having meaningful conversations about the important things that are happening in our life. Both men and women highly value the sense that we know details about our past and current activities and priorities, as well as what we are working towards in the future[42]. If we don't take a structured approach to this, we are simply leaving it to chance.

In the same way we bond with our children or with our pets, we can also bond with our partner. As mammals we have this keen sense of connection or love with others that isn't shared by all animals such as reptiles. This is based on the function in our bodies of the bonding chemical oxytocin[43], and is something that we can put to beneficial use in our relationship. Not only does this bring us closer to our partner but it works against the effects of dopamine which can lead to the emotional highs and lows that we can experience during Romantic Love.

For a stable and loving long term relationship we may find that the passionate fireworks of the first stage of the relationship do not provide the most solid and stable foundation to build something that will support us in the long term! Therefore, the development of these bonding rituals can be a powerful antidote to the highs and lows of the emotional rollercoaster. This is something that we cover during our work with couples, and usually requires some other foundations to be in place initially. For instance, if we are feeling a lot of negativity or

---

[42] John Gottman, The Seven Principles for Making Marriage Work
[43] Marnia Robinson, Cupid's Poisoned Arrow

232

resentment then we may not WANT to do the kinds of
simple exercises that can build this type of connection!

Conclusion

Working together with your partner

If we are looking for a solution together with our partner,
then having a process where we are both involved
would surely give us a better chance of finding a
solution that we can both buy into. This is why we often
work with couples looking to overcome a key challenge
or just to take their relationship to the next level. Sure,
you could sit down with a therapist but as the
differences between men and women is often one of the
key challenges that we work through, it's difficult for that
not to feel one-sided to one or other of us.

Even when the therapist is doing their best to be neutral,
it's very difficult for their own perception and style - as a
man or as a woman - to impact on the flavour of the
sessions. At that point, one partner may disengage -
even unconsciously - and feel that they are not being
heard and thus this is not for them.

Seeing both sides of the challenge

Imagine if one partner's issue is that they are forever
tidying and picking things up around the house. They
are busy and are getting frustrated that they are

spending their time tidying up after the other person and want to break that cycle. What if their partner accepts that they are messier, and for any number of reasons, leaves things lying around the home before getting around to tidying them away.

"But I was coming back to do that, I was just in a rush to go out to work so didn't have a chance to finish what I was doing", they may respond. "When I came back it was done!"

In this example there is a kind of fit between the two where the "messy one" and the "tidier one" cannot fully make sense of their pattern in isolation from the pattern or behaviour of their partner!

These dynamics come up all the time in the work we do, and why in general it's useful to at least begin the process together where your partner is open to that.

Doing the work on your own

In some cases, it may be either impractical or undesirable to work together with a partner. Sometimes a person may not currently be in a relationship but still feel that there are challenges from the past that need to be addressed.

"Maybe if I can get a handle on that thing now, I'm not going to mess things up again in the future," we might think to ourselves.

Or we may find ourselves with a partner who is less motivated or keen compared to ourselves to improve the relationship. In this situation we've got a really important decision to take, and it's one that ultimately does not depend on our partner. The question to consider is whether we may have an issue, but that our partner does not or at least that they are not actively looking to solve whatever challenge that may be.

Our needs versus our partner's needs

Once we've considered what our current unmet needs are, it is useful to reflect on the same question with respect to our partner. We could ask them directly if that is appropriate, or just to simply consider what is the evidence of the matter based on what we have directly observed. Often, we find that the needs that our partner is meeting through the relationship are completely different to the ones that we are looking to meet.

In my own case, my ex-partner's priorities for the relationship seemed to be in the areas of security and safety. It was important to her that everything was paid, the car was always full of petrol and that she received the payment of her allowance every month to cover her own expenditure. The holidays needed to be covered and the cupboards full of food. Beyond that, there was little engagement or interest. Fair enough, right?

The issue for me was that I was expecting to meet emotional needs of love and connection through my relationship, and my efforts to build bridges in this area seemed to be ignored. In this case we could say that there is no "ultimate" right and wrong about the purpose of the relationship but what we had was a mismatch in terms of our expectations which led to conflict.

Are things sustainable how they currently are?

The only viable assumption that we can make regarding our partner and our relationship is that unless otherwise addressed by ourselves, that things will continue to be exactly the way they are right now, for the rest of our lives.

If for any number of reasons this doesn't sound like an acceptable outcome, then we need to be ready to take some form of action to address things. We may have a clear idea of what we want, or we may simply know that what we currently have is not it. And we can't yet see a clear path through to the other side, partly because we are too close to the problem to have proper perspective. That's all ok for now because the mindset shift that starts the process is key.

We don't know what the answer is at this point, but we start to see that an answer is possible. And even more, we start to believe and commit to finding that answer whatever it takes. It goes from becoming a nice-to-have to becoming a MUST.

Making a loving invitation to our partner...

At this point we can make a positive invitation to our partner.

"Look, this is so important to me, and I really want things to work better. I'm committed to this journey and showing up as best I can to make this relationship work," we could say.

It's extremely unlikely that making this kind of invitation is ever going to be a breach of boundary. We are simply asking the question and detaching from the outcome. Remember that whether the person accepts or declines the invitation is their business! We need to diligently avoid any kind of guilt tripping, manipulation, or threat at this point. There is no sense that they "should" say yes (or no), as whatever they say is up to them!

While being clear that this is happening anyway!

The key to remaining empowered at this point, is to convey a crucial point. We might say this explicitly or leave it clear through our tonality. That is that whether they join us or not, that we ourselves are committed to making a change. It's either going to be a process that we enter together or if necessary, it's one we are going on our own. So long as this is stated in a positive matter-of-fact way there is no sense of threat or control at all.

Whether our partner wants to join us in this work is their business. But the decision for ourselves about whether we want to work on things is our business. If we make our participation or look for support contingent on their agreement, who has the power in the decision?

"No, I can't work on things myself, without their agreement/ participation," is a breach of boundaries based on what we have explored.

Because with this statement we are making our business (working on ourselves), someone else's business (giving our partner the veto). If we adopt such a position, how are we likely to make ourselves feel - empowered or disempowered?

The one person we can work on

As we say there is only one person we can really work on here in any case. That person is us! The best starting point is to say that we're ready to play all out, to focus on our part of things and to trust that our partner will do likewise in whatever way is right for them. Not everyone is ready to take responsibility in this sense, but all we can really do is look at how we ourselves have contributed to or perpetuated the process.

On the plus side is that when we do step up and get ourselves into the best possible place, we'll be ready to deal with whatever challenges we need to work on. Our partner will decide to join, or they won't. However, it's much more likely that they may decide to act if we simply step up and lead by example, rather than waiting and hoping that something will change. It's extremely unlikely that any form of nagging or expectation will move our partner towards action. In fact, it's likely to do the exact opposite.

Moving towards a dream of a better relationship

"Everyone argues anyway, and no relationship really works", people sometimes say. It's like there's this idea in our culture that no matter what we do, they are just fundamentally doomed to remain an enigma, like an uncrackable code! This statement is a fitting example of a disempowering assumption that is unprovable. To KNOW this was the case we'd need to somehow review or survey every relationship that there is and ever was and gather some kind of objective data! If anyone fancies taking that on, please let me know!

So, what's the alternative? And what would it take to buy into it? In our work we have the advantage of seeing with our own eyes what happens when people finally get to the point of saying that things can't go on the way they are, and that something must change. We typically meet people when they've hit rock bottom and support them to make sense of things and piece them back together. So, we couldn't buy into this disempowering sense of giving up even if we wanted to!

How about if we believed that with a clearer understanding and consistent application of proven strategies that improvement was not only possible, but inevitable. It's like trying to get fit - if we do the work, we can 100% guarantee that we will see improvement. The question is whether we choose to do that work or not.

Should I stay or should I go?

Sometimes we already know the answer to our relationship challenge, although we've been spending time and energy wishing we didn't know. If we want to experience a great relationship, and our partner is not interested in supporting us in moving towards that, it's worth considering what that is telling us.

It's also worth remembering that there are always things that we can address solely from our side, that when addressed can fundamentally improve our situation. That improvement may result in the relationship changing, or in our relationship situation changing and this is something that we can remain totally responsible for. Often through that journey the relationship itself is transformed, but either way we'll be in a much better position to build a life that works for us and the people around us, whether our partner chooses to be a part of that life. We might even choose that WE wouldn't want them to be a part of it after all!

When the gap feels insurmountable

Sometimes when the relationship has been challenging for some time, and strong resentment has set in it can be a difficult journey to recapturing anything worthwhile. It's like over time life has been sucked out of us, and we can't envisage any way of reclaiming a functional relationship from the rubble. Only we can decide whether we've reached a point of no return where any work on the relationship would feel like a waste of time.

Re-building on proper foundations

For many couples though, once the builders have been in and fixed the metaphorical foundations, any re-building we do from that point onwards has a vastly different quality that anything we were trying to paper over beforehand. In a sense, until we have done that work or at least made some initial investigations we are premature in wanting to abandon the house. Let's have a look first, then when we've scoped it, we can decide whether we are willing and able to put in the work required to make it safe then strong again.

Getting the support you need

It is sometimes said that our destiny is shaped in our moments of decision, and deciding about how best to resolve our relationship challenge is one of those forks in the road that can lead us to a vastly different place. Once we choose a path, the option of retracing our steps and changing our mind may not be a straightforward process. Even if we come back to that point, the other road may be closed or blocked by the time we get there.

So, we are right to take proper care and consideration as we stand at that fork to really weigh up our options before making a move down that road.

Well done for taking the time to read this book, and for starting to consider a decision that can lead you to a fundamentally different destination to the path that you are currently on!

About the Author

Matt Albiges is a relationship expert, therapist and educator who works with his wife Rebeca Perea with couples and individuals to create relationships that really serve them and the people around them.

He is the host of The Relationship Breakthrough Show with Matt & Rebeca podcast that is available of all major podcasting platforms and has been featured regularly on regional and national media including GB News and the BBC.

He is also regularly invited to address audiences from the stage or through online events including internationally.

If you are looking for instant tailored feedback on your relationship situation why not start with the Relationship CLARITY Scorecard which can be accessed from the homepage of the website. In just a few minutes you can answer some simple YES/NO questions to see where you are currently doing well and the areas that would benefit from addressing:

www.alignedwithlove.net